MAKE YOUR OWN M
DINOSAURS

By Danny A. Downs

with Tom Knight

Fox
Chapel Publishing

1970 Broad Street • East Petersburg, PA 17520
www.FoxChapelPublishing.com

Publisher	Alan Giagnocavo
Editor	Ayleen Stellhorn
Editorial Assistant	Gretchen Bacon
Cover Design	Jon Deck
Layout	Leah Smirlis

ISBN 1-56523-244-5

Library of Congress Control Number: 2004106142

To order your copy of this book,
please send check or money order
for the cover price plus $3.50 shipping to:
Fox Chapel Publishing
Book Orders
1970 Broad St.
East Petersburg, PA 17520

Or visit us on the Web at **www.FoxChapelPublishing.com**

Printed in China
10 9 8 7 6 5 4 3 2 1

Contents

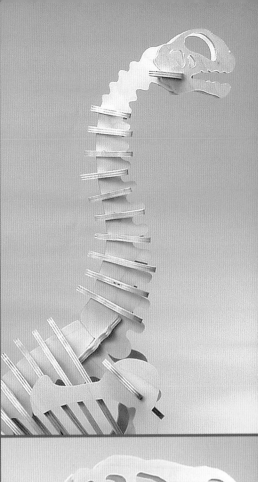
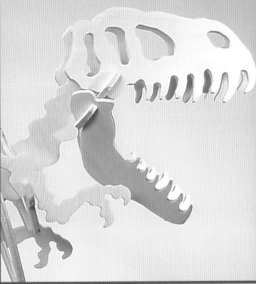
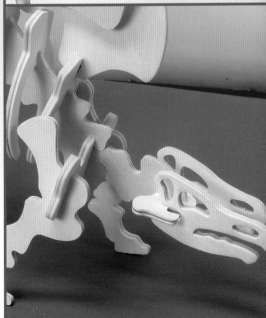

About the Author

Dan Downs was one of the founding partners of B.C. Bones. He is heavily involved in the woodworking industry and currently runs a contract manufacturing facility utilizing CNC (computer numeric controlled) routing technology. You can visit him on the web at **www.thecncshop.com**. Dan lives in Northern California with his wife and two children.

The patterns in this book have been used to produce more than a half-million dinosaur puzzles. B.C. Bones puzzles have been featured in numerous catalogs and toy and speciality stores around the world, and are currently distributed by The Toysmith Company in Auburn, Washington. These patterns are still in use today to produce the B.C. Bones product line and are used regularly at his manufacturing facility.

Acknowledgements:

Special thanks to Dale Whisler and the members of the Tri-County Scrollers for cutting the model dinosaurs pictured in this book.

CUTTING DINOSAUR MODELS ON YOUR SCROLL SAW

Dinosaurs have fascinated modern man ever since the first dinosaur bones were discovered nearly 200 years ago. Nothing stretches our imagination and our sense of wonder like the thought of a beast larger than a two-story house and fiercer than the number of lions it would take to fill that house.

But even with as much as we've learned about dinosaurs over the past two centuries, we have only begun to scratch the surface of their world and their daily lives. Skeletal remains—in most cases, incomplete skeletal remains—can help scientists to discern many things like weight, height and general diet, but much is unknown. What kinds of sounds did dinosaurs make? What colors were they? How long did they care for their young?

Where science tapers off, imagination picks up.

Scroll Saw Skeletons

Science was the driving force behind the creation of the seven scroll saw dinosaur skeletons included in this book. Much research went into studying the skeletal remains of dinosaurs. As a result, the model skeletons presented here are reasonably accurate. The overall posture and bone structure is correct according to museum displays. However, creative liberties were taken with the number and scale of the bones. This was necessary to create a workable pattern that could be cut on a scroll saw.

Material Choice

From this point, imagination takes over. The scroll saw is a versatile tool, able to cut a variety of materials. All of the models in the pattern section of this book were cut from cabinet-grade plywood. This type of plywood can be left unfinished for a light tan, almost-bone color, or it can be stained to resemble cherry, walnut, pecan or any number of hardwoods. The pieces can also be painted; however, frequent disassembly and reassembly will cause the paint at the joints to wear and flake.

A second option is to cut the skeletons from hardwood. Walnut and cherry are highly recommended. The tight grain of these woods makes them ideal choices for these patterns. Woods with a coarse grain, such as oak, should be avoided. The coarse grain cannot support the weight and balance point of the assembled dinosaur; it becomes brittle and has a tendency to break.

A third option is to try a non-wood material such as Corian (commonly used for kitchen and bathroom countertops) or Plexiglas. Both of these materials come in a wide variety of colors, which can produce some spectacular results.

Pattern Use

The patterns in this book are supplied at their actual size and are arranged to fit a 17" x 11" board. Because each of the pattern pieces fit together with $1/4$" interlocking joints, it is important that the thickness of the material you choose is exactly $1/4$". Many times, $1/4$"-inch-thick wood actually measures slightly less than $1/4$". Be sure to measure the thickness of the material prior to cutting the pieces. If the material is slightly larger or slightly smaller than the notches on the patterns, adjust the notches to the exact thickness of the material.

Patterns can be affixed to the material in a variety of ways. In this book, I used double-sided tape. The tape is clean, easy to use and has a remarkably strong hold. Another possibility includes temporary spray adhesive (repositionable photo spray).

As you cut the pieces, do not remove the pattern. It is important to check the fit of the interlocking joint (see sidebar) and transfer the pattern numbers to the wood before removing the pattern.

Display

These model skeletons have two basic uses: display as a decorative item or use as an interactive toy.

If you choose to display your finished model as a decorative item, consider gluing the pieces together and affixing the assembled skeleton to a sturdy base. A glued dinosaur skeleton that tumbles from a shelf or desktop is prone to irreparable breakage. More expensive materials, such as hardwoods or Corian are ideal for display. As you assemble the piece, you can erase the numbers that are keyed to the interlocking joints.

If you choose to use your finished dinosaur as an interactive toy, be sure that the child (or adult) is over the age of 8. These models include some small pieces that may cause choking if swallowed by younger children. Also, be sure to choose a durable wood, such as cabinet-grade plywood, and a non-toxic finish. The numbers that are keyed to the interlocking joints can be left on the pieces or stamped into the wood to aid in assembly. Remove the numbers for a true challenge.

Plywood is soft enough that you can stamp the part numbers right into the wood. This method of marking the pieces is ideal for dinosaur models that will be disassembled and reassembled frequently—like those given as gifts to older children.

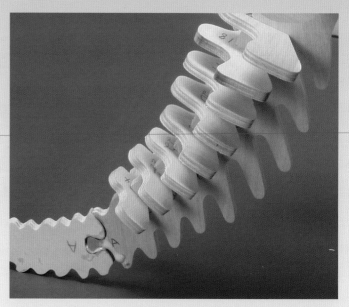

As you cut the pieces, be sure to transfer the part numbers to the wood. If you plan to apply a finish to the dinosaur, use pencil so the marks can be erased after assembly.

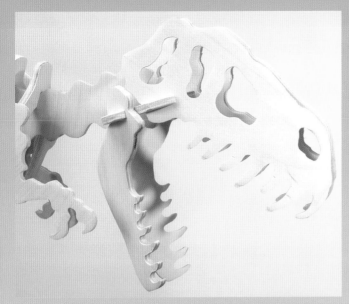

Several of the pattern pieces for most of the dinosaur models in this book can be stack cut because the pieces are exact duplicates. The skull and jawbone of the Tyrannosaurus Rex are two examples. See the individual patterns for lists of pieces to stack cut.

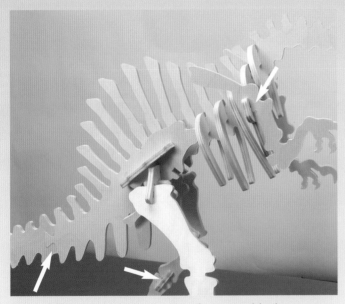

Three different connectors are used to assemble the pieces (from left to right): puzzle keys, double tab connectors, and single tab connectors.

Tips

• Affix the pattern to an 11" x 17" board, then cut it down into several smaller pieces before you begin to cut the patterns. This will give you more control over the board and increase the accuracy of your cuts.

• Use a #3 scroll saw blade. This blade is easier to control than a #5.

• Use a $\frac{1}{16}$" drill bit to drill starter holes for the inside cuts.

• If the pattern overhangs the edge of the board, trim it back with your scroll saw. Your fingers can slip if you grab paper when you are expecting to grab wood.

• Save time by stack cutting identical pieces (see page 8).

• Hide the start of your cut in a nook or curve of the pattern. An inconspicuous start will help you to end up with a smooth finished piece.

• Cut at a slow, steady pace, but don't cut so slow that you burn the wood.

• Beginners may want to cut the outlines first, then return to cut the notches in a second pass.

• Double-check the width of the joints on the patterns against the width of the wood before you begin to cut. Wood that is sold as $\frac{1}{4}$" plywood often measures slightly less in thickness.

• Check the joints again after they are cut by test-fitting the joint with a piece of scrap wood.

• Transfer the numbers on the pattern to the wood before you remove the pattern. These numbers are key to assembling the dinosaur correctly.

• Mark the pattern numbers lightly with a pencil if you plan to remove them later; stamp them into the wood if the model will be disassembled and reassembled frequently.

• Enlarge or reduce the patterns to create table top or room-sized dinosaurs. Remember that the tabs will need to be redrawn by hand to match the width of the wood.

Cutting Perfect Tabs

Cutting the tabs by which the pieces are connected may look like a daunting task, especially to a beginner. The photos below—and some practice on a piece of scrap wood—will help you learn to make perfect tabs.

Always cut to the outside of the pattern line. Cutting to the outside will make the tab just a little too narrow, making the fit very tight. Cutting to the inside of the lines will make the fit too loose, making it necessary to recut the entire piece. Test fit the tab with a small piece of waste wood. If the fit is too tight, simply remove a small portion of wood with the scroll saw or with a piece of coarse sandpaper until the fit is perfect.

Cutting Perfect Corners

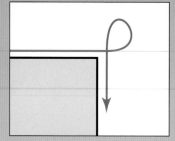
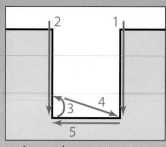

Use a looping cut to make outside corners.

Make inside corners with several cuts.

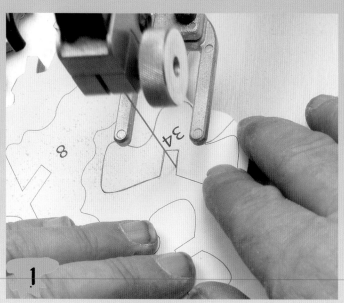

Cut to the outside of the pattern line.

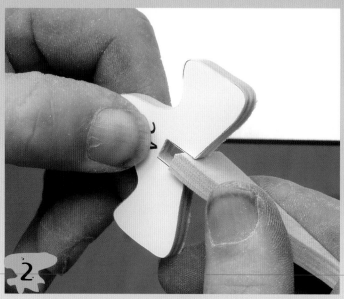

Test the fit with a piece of waste wood.

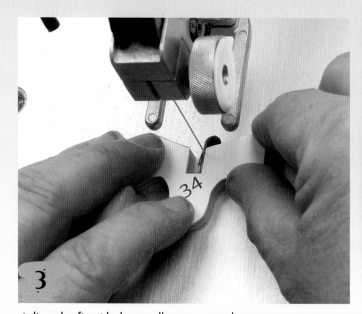

Adjust the fit with the scroll saw or sandpaper.

A perfect fit.

Tyrannosaurus

DINO FACTS

TYRANNOSAURUS
(tie-RAN-oh-sawr-us)

- Meat eater
- Name means "tyrant lizard"
- Size: 18 feet tall, 46 feet long
- Weight: 6 tons
- Lived near the end of the Cretaceous
- Bones found in western Canada and western United States

Tyrannosaurus Rex Cutting Demonstration

MATERIALS

Double-sided tape
Cabinet-grade plywood
   (4 pieces at 11" x 17" x ¹/₄")
Copies of the pattern (1 copy of each pattern)
#3 regular scroll saw blade

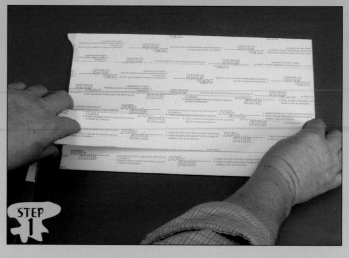

STEP 1

Remove the backing from one side of a strip of double-sided tape. Apply the tape, in slightly overlapping rows, to a piece of 11" x 17" x ¹/₄" cabinet-grade plywood.

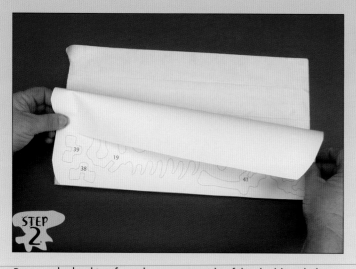

STEP 2

Remove the backing from the opposite side of the double-sided tape. Apply the pattern to the wood by matching up the bottom corner of the pattern first. Press diagonally, up and out, to ensure that the pattern doesn't wrinkle or bubble as it is applied.

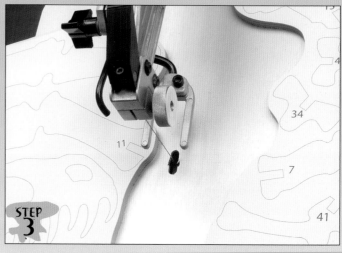

STEP 3

The throat of most scroll saws is too small to comfortably cut the 11" x 17" x ¹/₄" piece of plywood. Use the scroll saw to cut the plywood into smaller, more manageable pieces as shown.

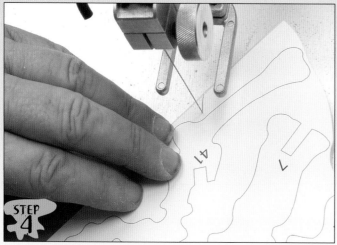

STEP 4

Decide which pattern piece to cut first. Here we chose a front leg (K). Cut into the wood, starting your cut at a non-intrusive spot. Curves and corners are ideal places to start your cuts.

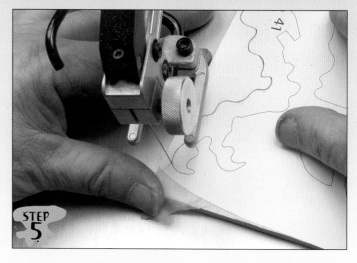

STEP 5

Continue cutting, following the line as precisely as possible. While it's true that slight deviations from the pattern lines won't be noticed when you remove the pattern, larger mistakes should be avoided because they will alter the balance of the assembled dinosaur.

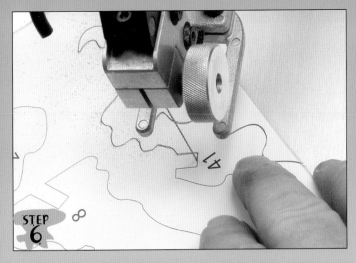

STEP 6

Cut the notch, staying to the outside of the line. (See the sidebar on page 4, Cutting Perfect Corners.)

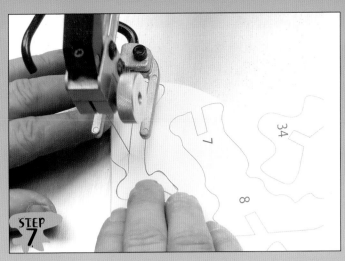

STEP 7

Complete the cut, making sure that the final cut matches perfectly with your starting cut.

STEP 8

Remove the scrolled piece from the plywood.

STEP 9

Check the fit of the notch by inserting a small waste piece of plywood. In this photo, the notch is just a bit too small. Note: Make sure that the paper pattern has been removed from the waste piece of wood. The added thickness of the paper will make the final fit too loose when the paper is removed.

STEP 10

Re-cut the notch with the scroll saw, removing only very small amounts of wood at a time. If the notch is only slightly too small, run a piece of coarse sandpaper along the inside edge of the cut to remove additional wood.

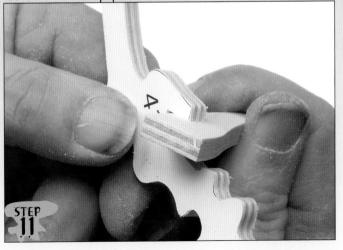

STEP 11

Recheck the fit frequently until it is perfect. Cut the remaining pattern pieces in the same manner, transferring the numbers to the wood as your remove the patterns.

Time Saver: Stack Cutting Individual Pieces

Stack cutting refers to cutting the same pattern from multiple pieces of wood at the same time. Each dinosaur pattern in this book has at least several pattern pieces that can be stack cut. Refer to each individual dinosaur pattern for a list of duplicate pieces.

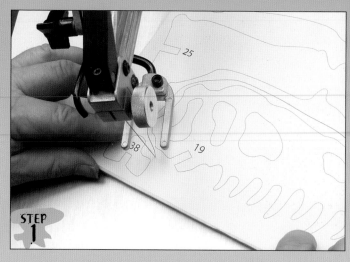

STEP 1

The skull is one of four pattern pieces that can be stack cut from the Tyrannosaurus Rex pattern. Use the scroll saw to roughly cut the piece of plywood down to size.

STEP 2

Place the rough-cut skull on a second piece of plywood and trace around the edges.

STEP 3

Use the scroll saw to cut the traced piece from the second piece of plywood.

STEP 4

Remove the backing from a strip of double-sided tape and apply it to the face of the wood you cut in Step 3. One strip across the center of the piece is all you will need to hold the two pieces securely together.

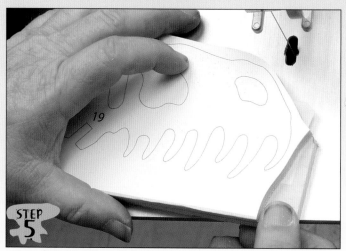

STEP 5

Line up the two pieces and press them together.

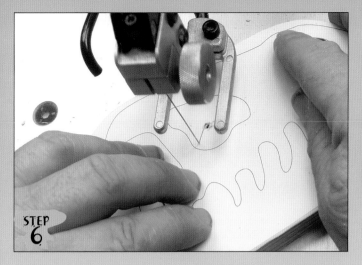

STEP 6

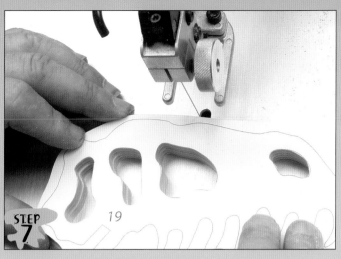

STEP 7

Using a portable drill with a 1/16" bit, drill the starter holes for any interior cuts. Insert the blade through the starter hole and begin cutting the frets.

Make all of the inside cuts before you move on to the outside cut. In this photo all of the frets in the skull have been cut.

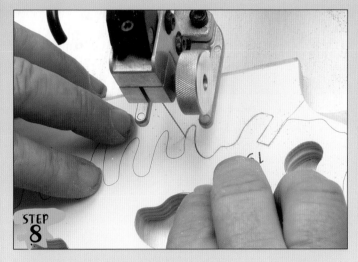

STEP 8

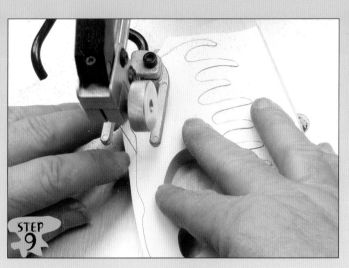

STEP 9

Cut in at an inconspicuous spot and follow the line as precisely as possible. Remember to stay to the outside of the line when cutting the tabs.

Continue cutting the outline of the skull.

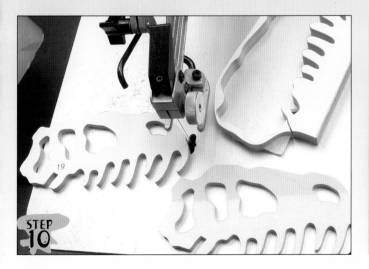

STEP 10

STEP 11

Separate the cut pieces from the waste wood. Transfer any numbers on the pattern to the wood.

Check the fit of the tab by inserting a piece of waste wood. Here the fit is too tight. To adjust the fit, remove a small amount of wood with the scroll saw blade or a piece of sand paper. Continue cutting the remaining stack cut pieces according to the list on the pattern.

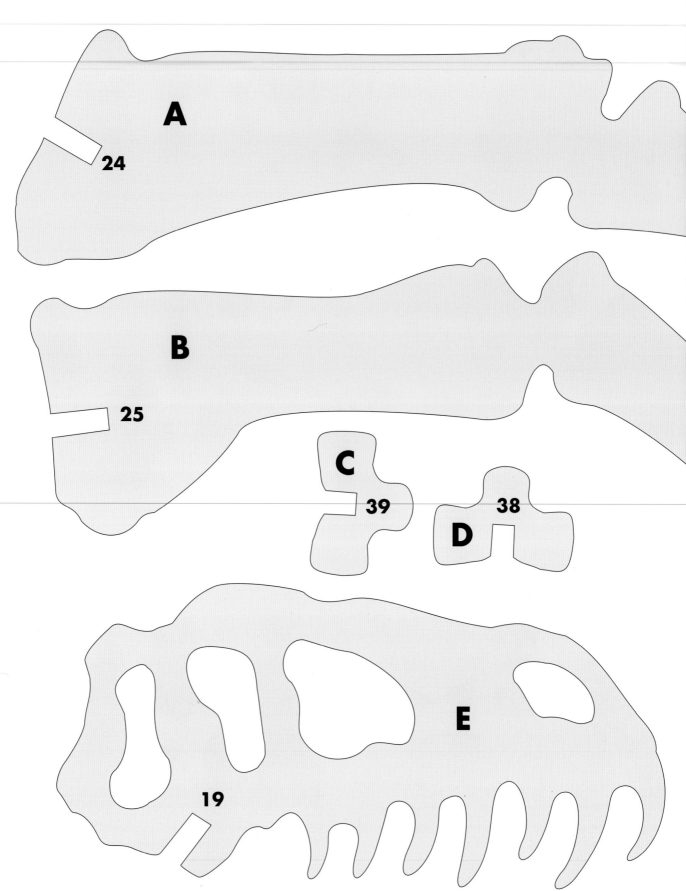

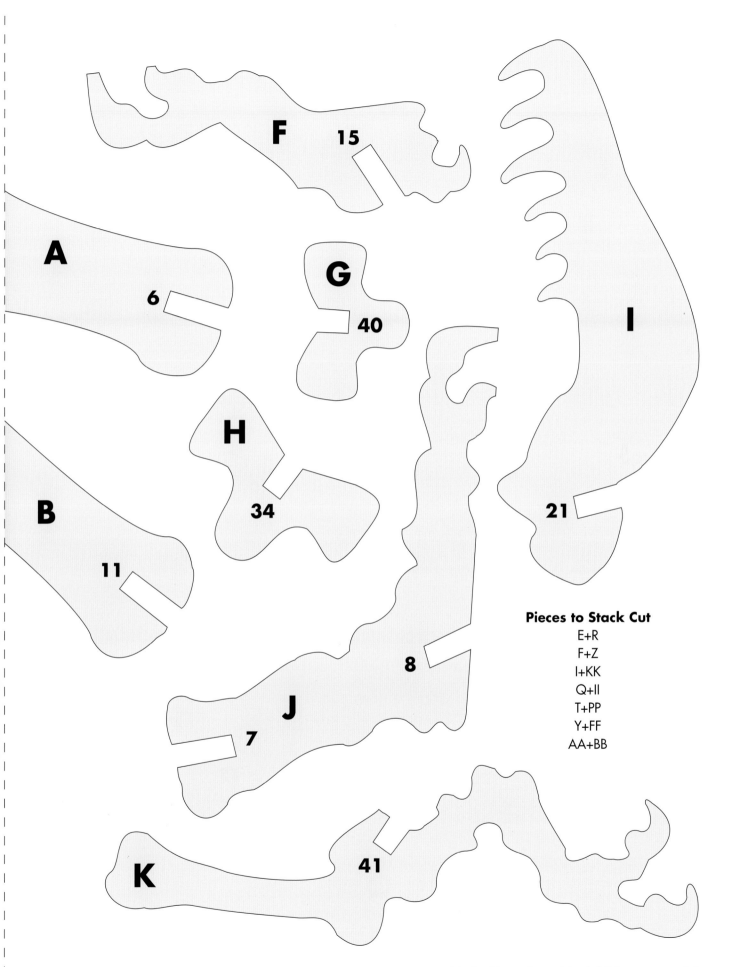

Pieces to Stack Cut
E+R
F+Z
I+KK
Q+II
T+PP
Y+FF
AA+BB

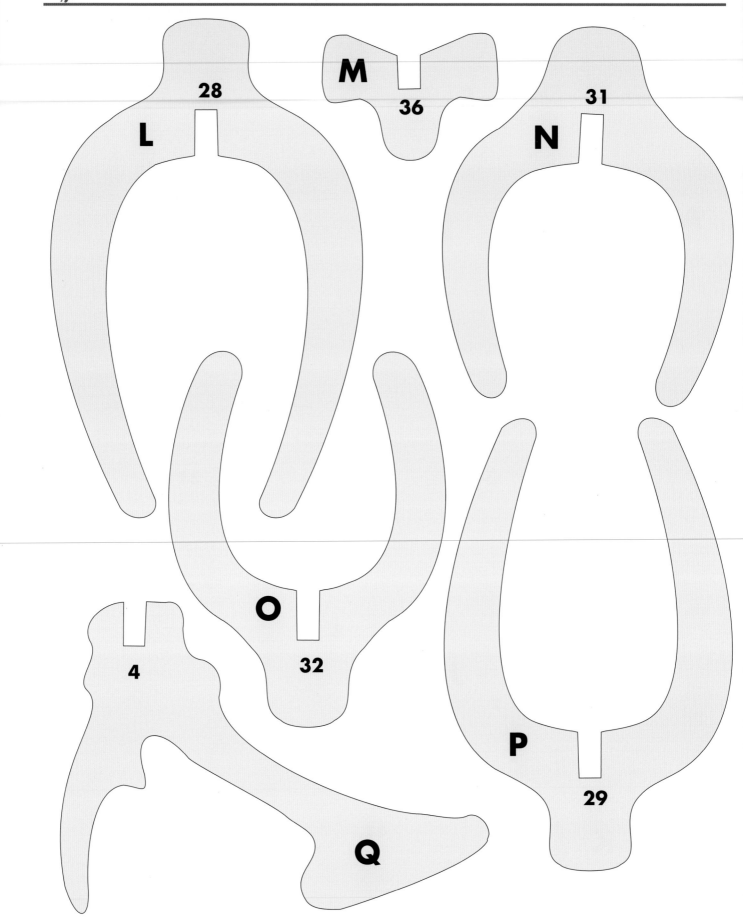

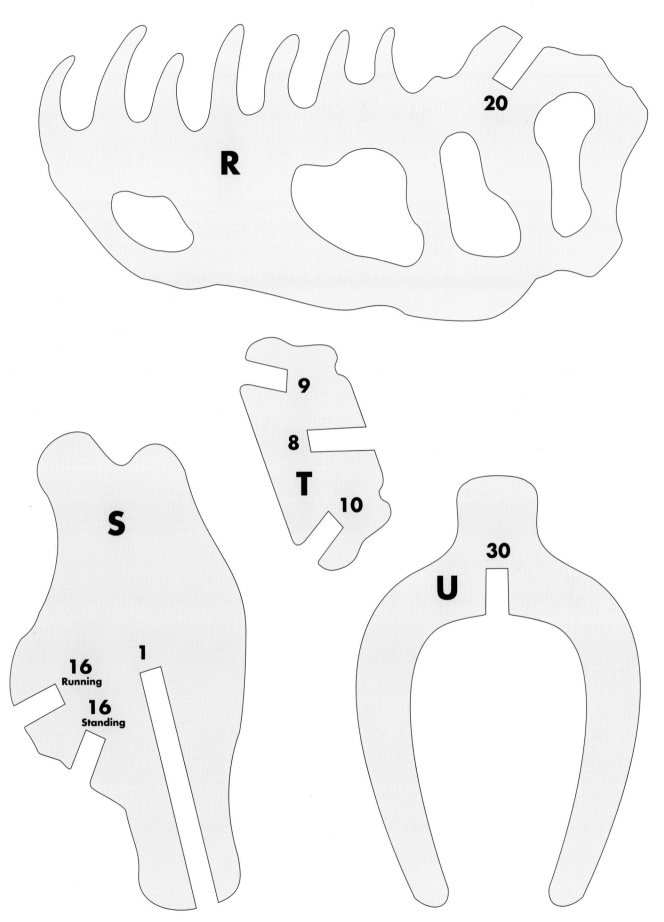

R

20

9

8

T

10

S

16
Running

16
Standing

1

U

30

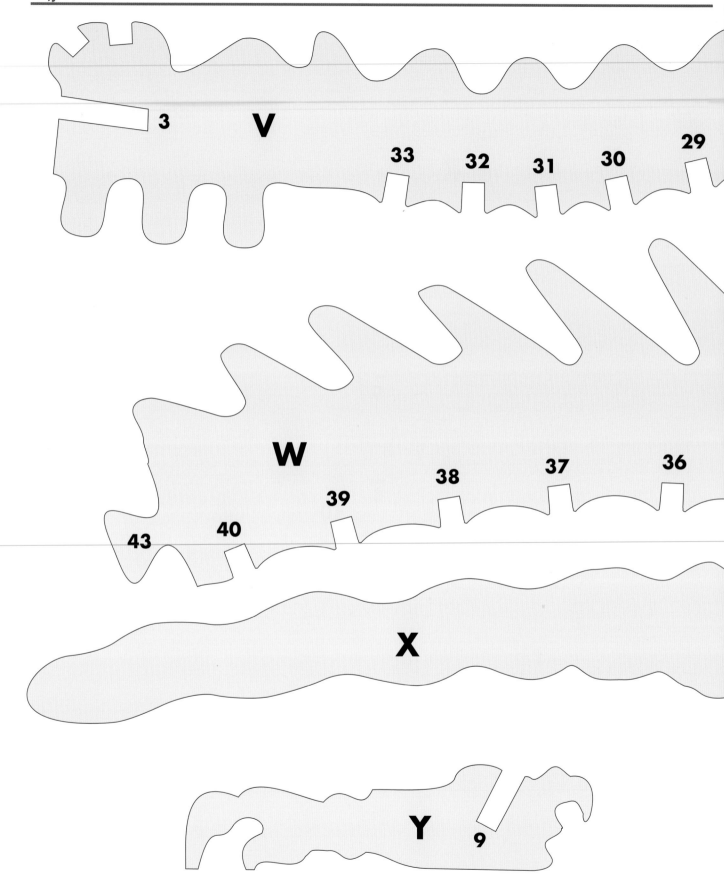

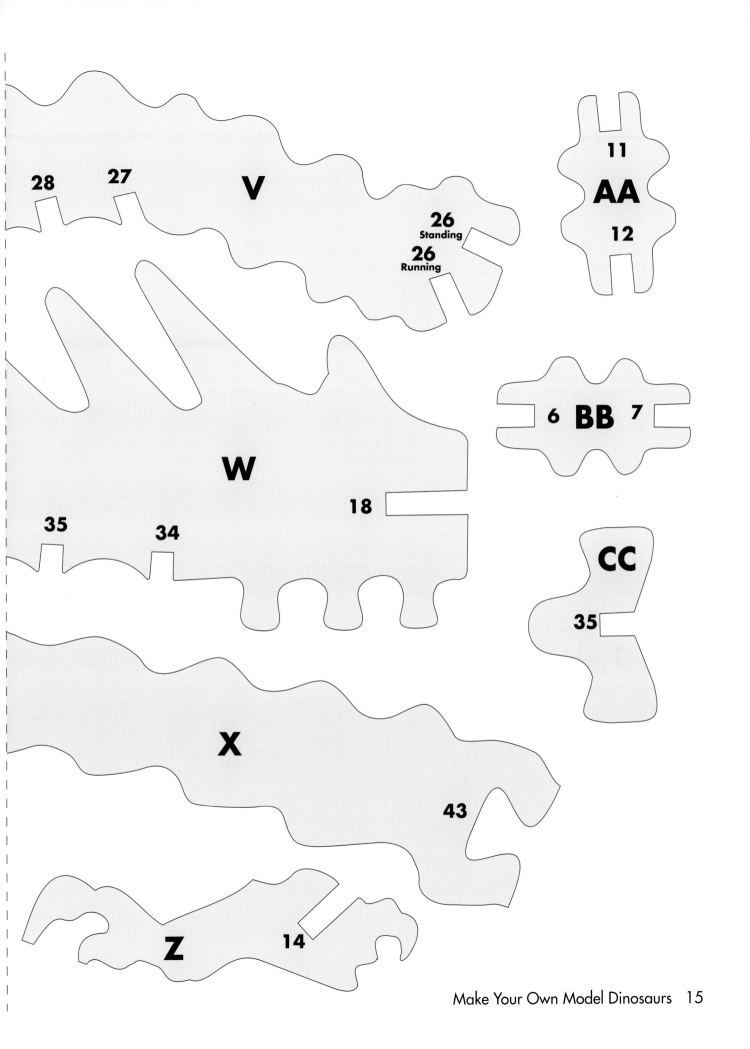

28   27   **V**

26
Standing

26
Running

11
AA
12

6 BB 7

W

18

35   34

CC

35

X

43

Z   14

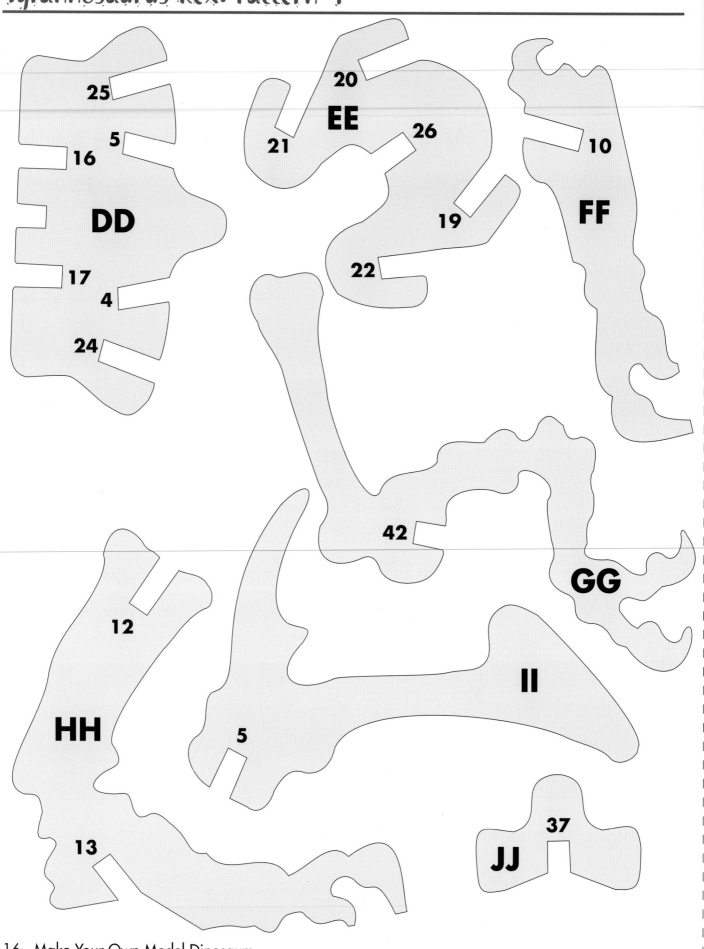

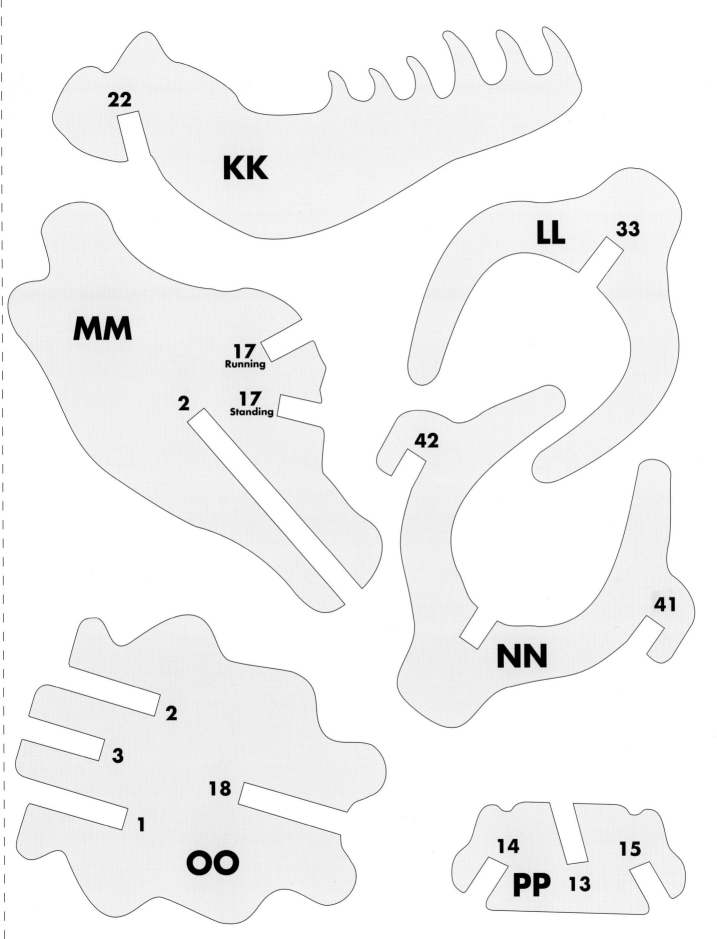

22

KK

MM

17
Running

17
Standing

2

LL   33

42

41

NN

2

3

18

1

OO

14   15

PP   13

Allosaurus

DINO FACTS

ALLOSAURUS
(AL-oh-sawr-us)

- Meat eater, bi-pedal
- Name means "other lizard"
- Size: 17 feet tall, 40 feet long
- Weight: 4,000 tons
- Lived in the late Jurassic
- Bones found in Utah

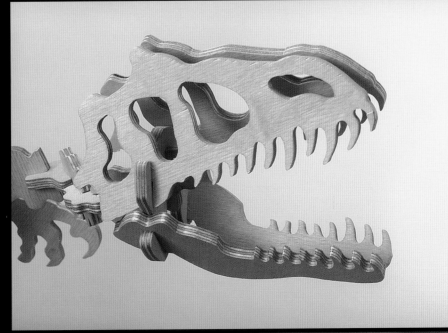

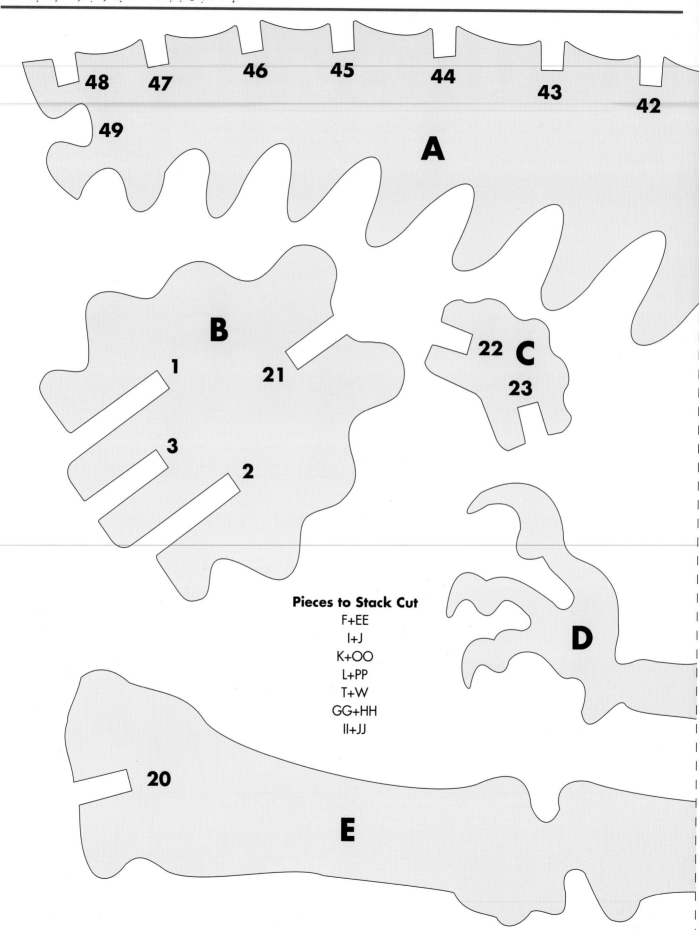

48 47 46 45 44 43 42

49

A

B

1 21

3

2

22 C

23

Pieces to Stack Cut
F+EE
I+J
K+OO
L+PP
T+W
GG+HH
II+JJ

D

20

E

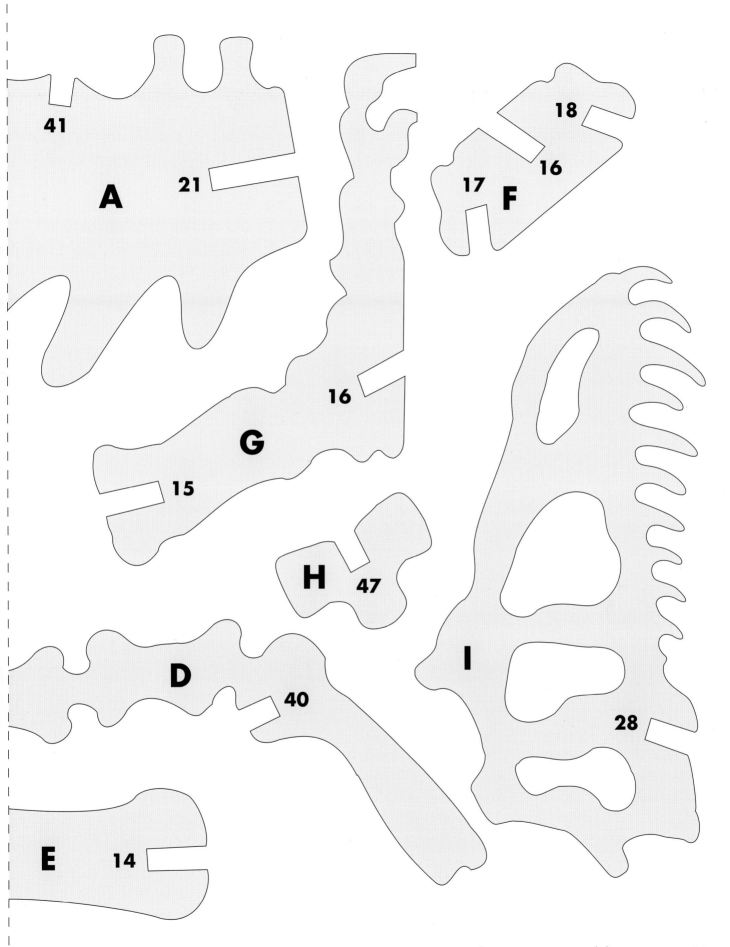

41

A

21

F

18

16

17

G

16

15

H

47

I

D

40

28

E

14

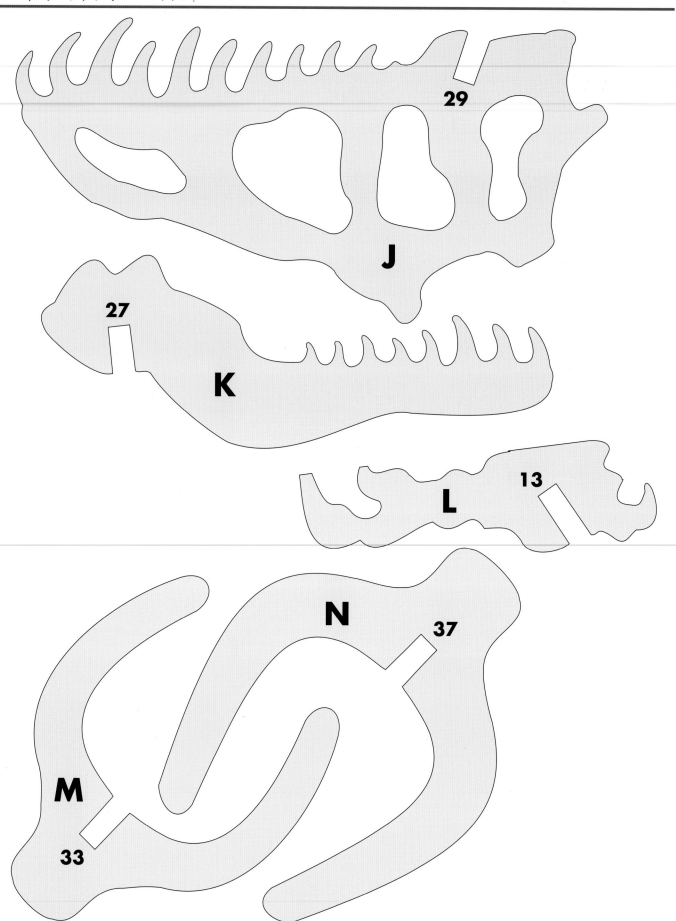

29

27

J

K

13

L

N

37

M

33

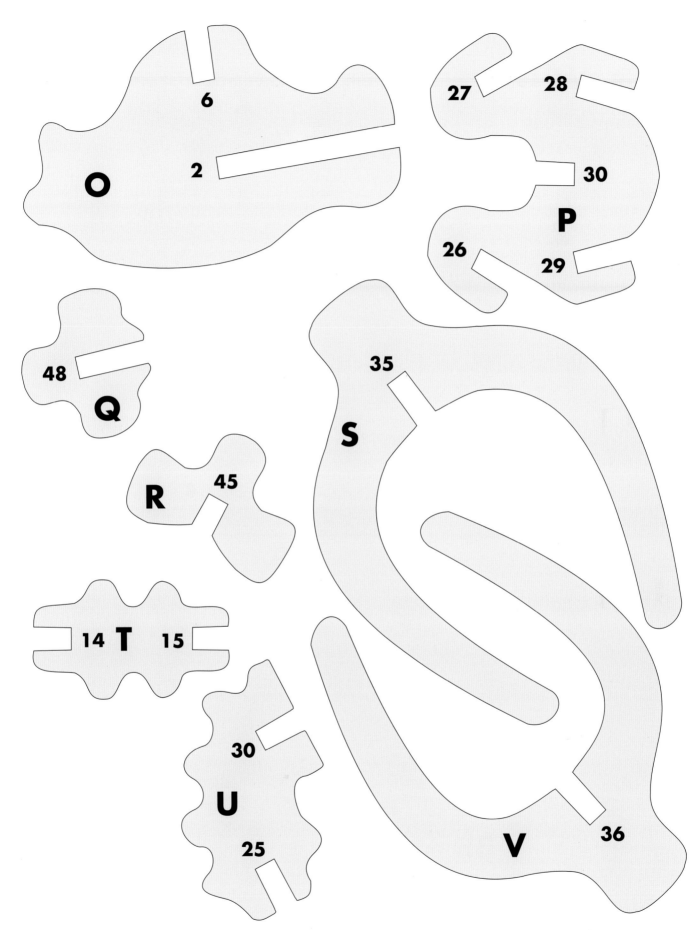

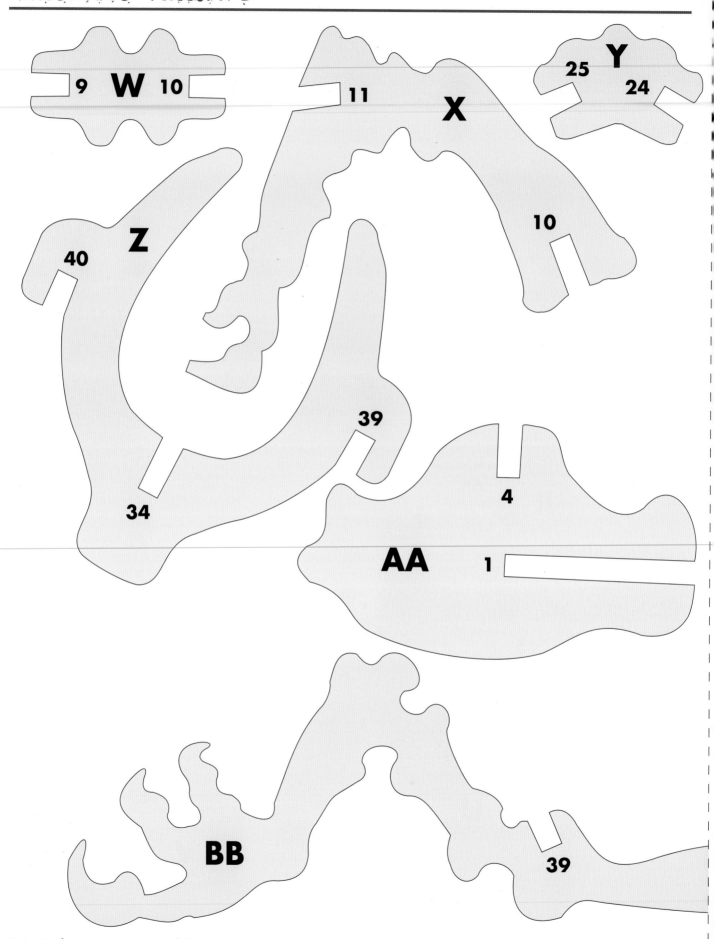

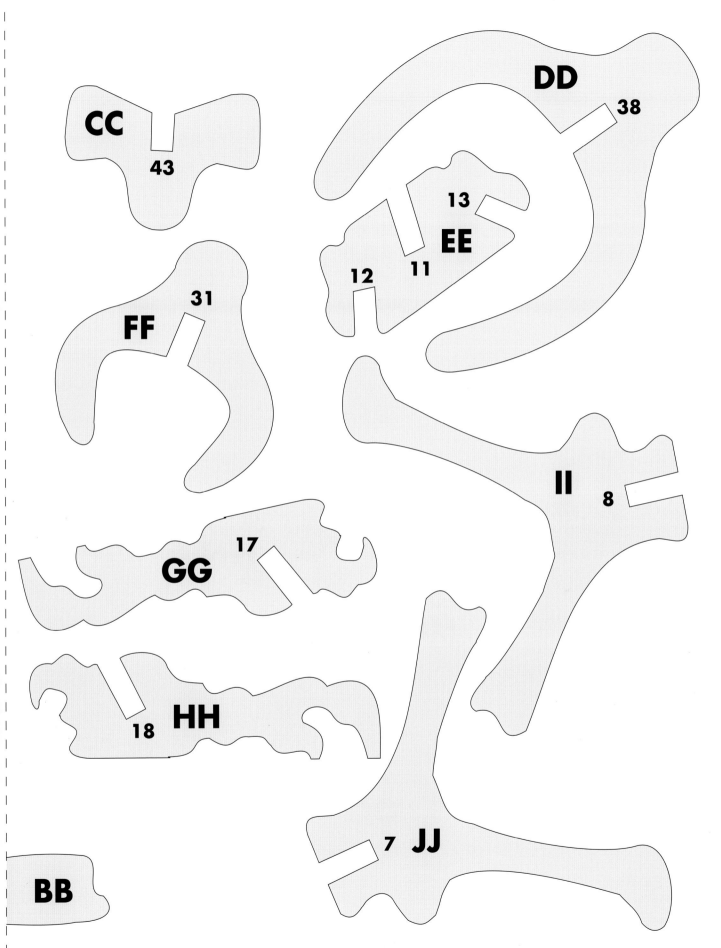

CC
43

DD
38

EE
13
12 11

FF
31

GG
17

II
8

HH
18

JJ
7

BB

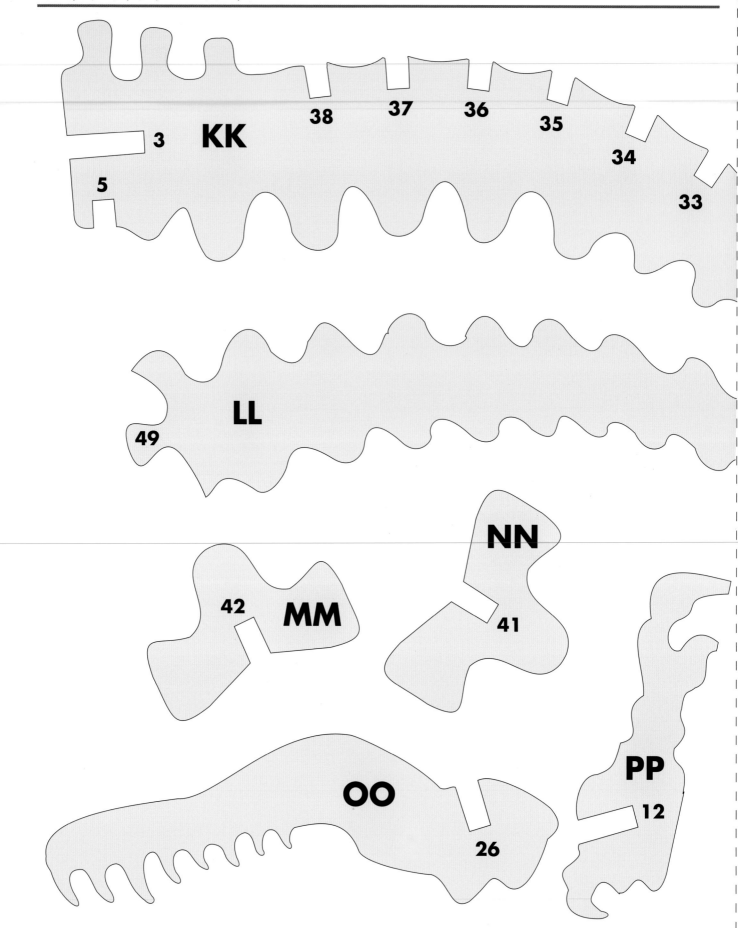

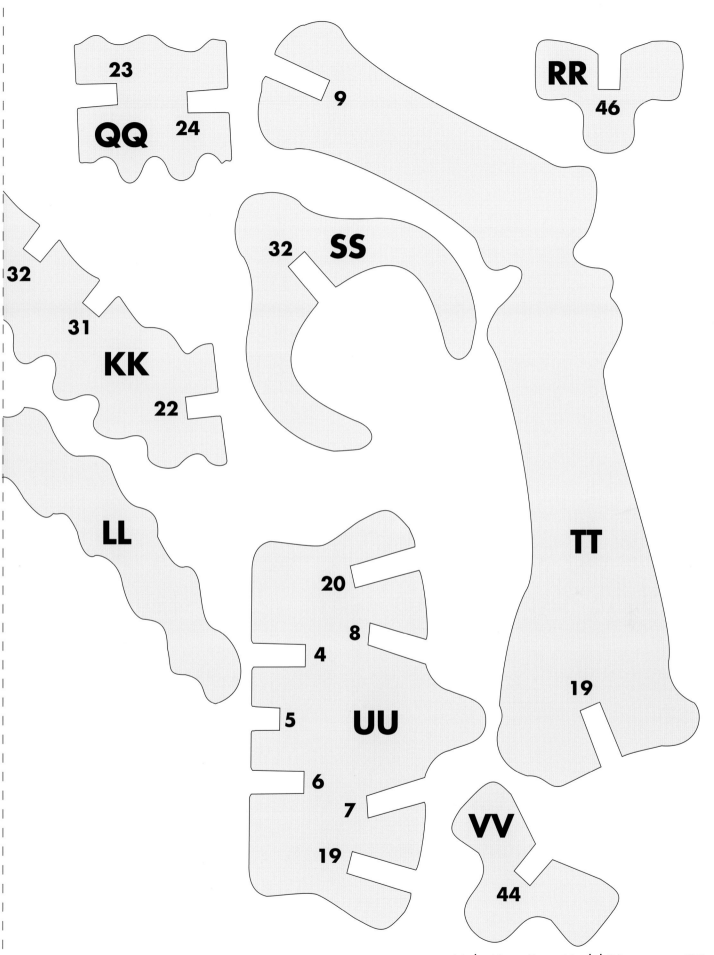

Allosaurus: Assembly Drawing

Jobaria

DINO FACTS

JOBARIA
(jo-BAR-e-ya)

- Plant eater, quadruped
- Size: 70 feet long, 30 feet tall on hind legs
- Weight: 40,000 pounds
- Lived during the Cretaceous
- Bones found in Niger, Africa

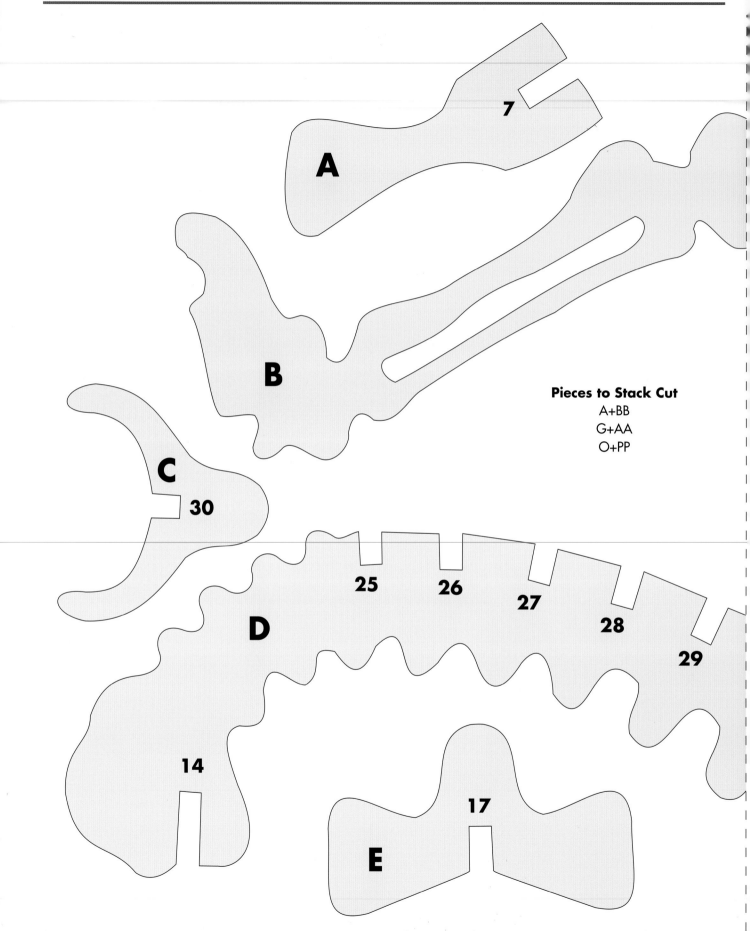

Pieces to Stack Cut
A+BB
G+AA
O+PP

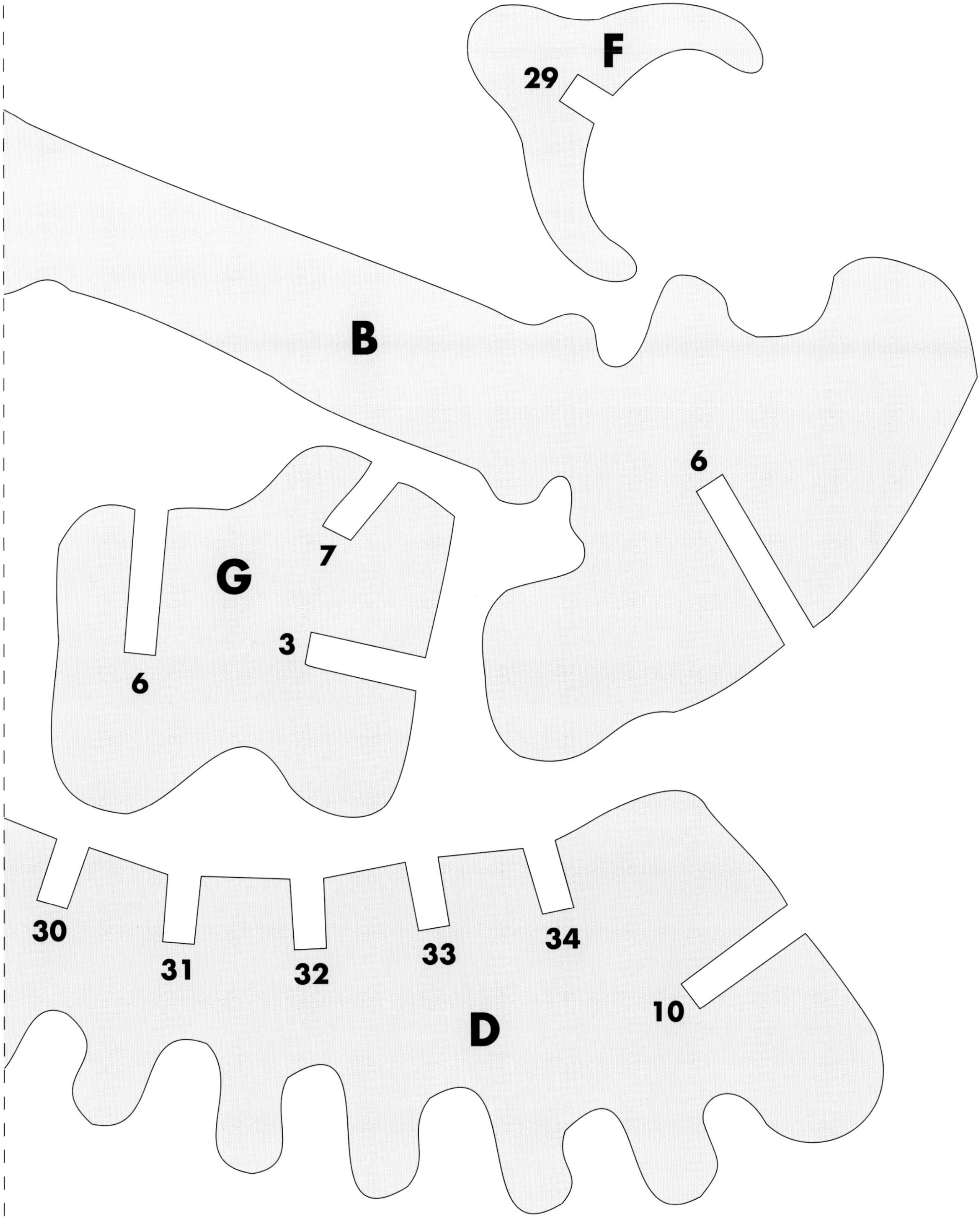
F
29
B
6
7
G
3
6
30
31
32
33
34
10
D

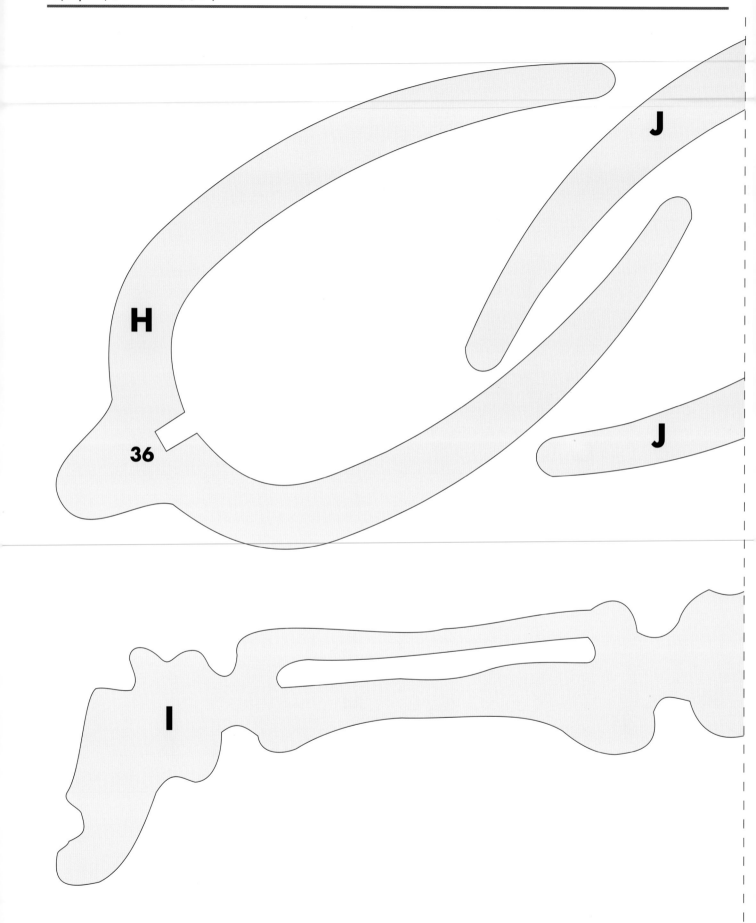

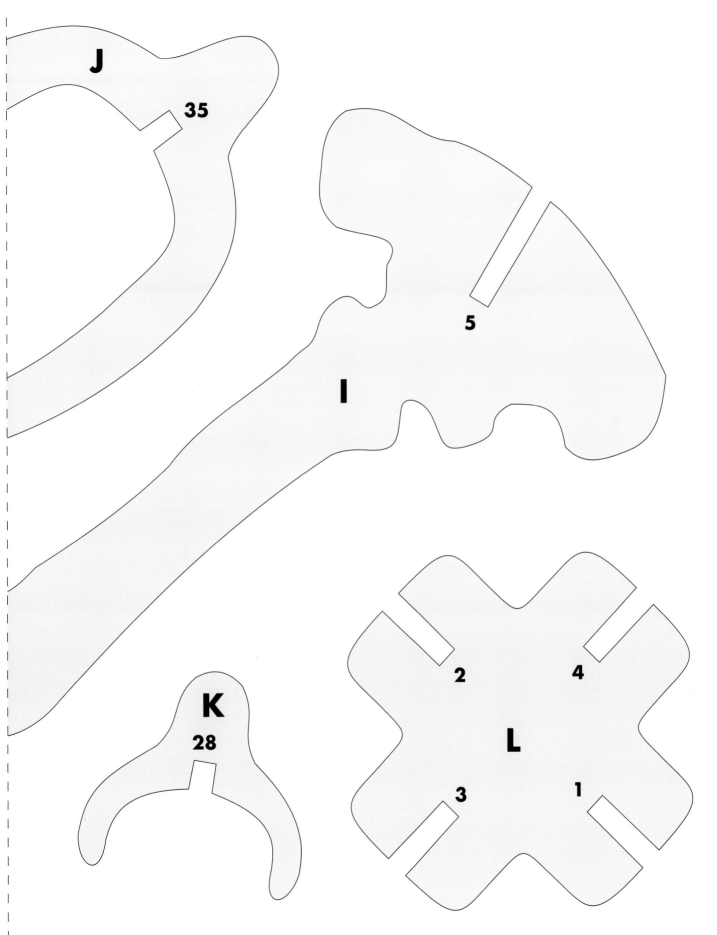

J

35

I

5

K

28

L

2

4

3

1

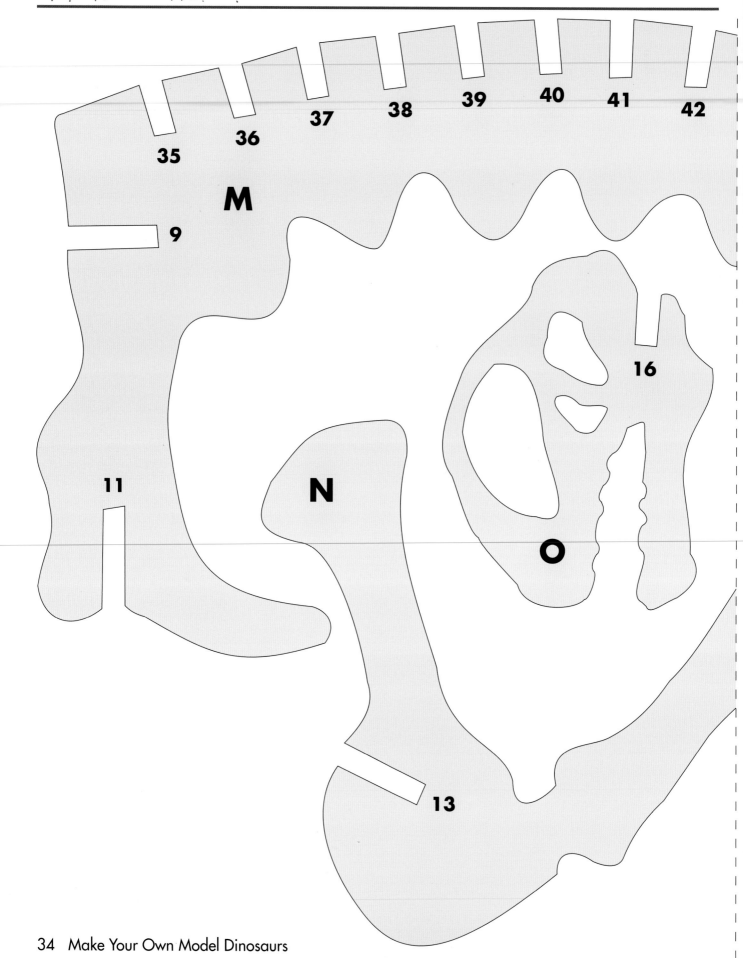

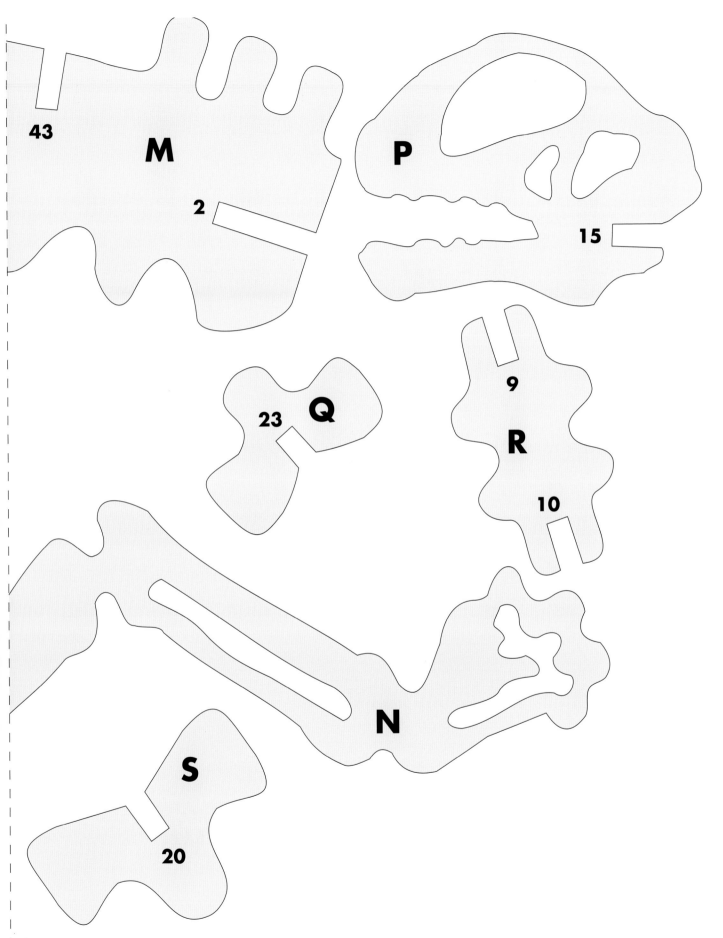

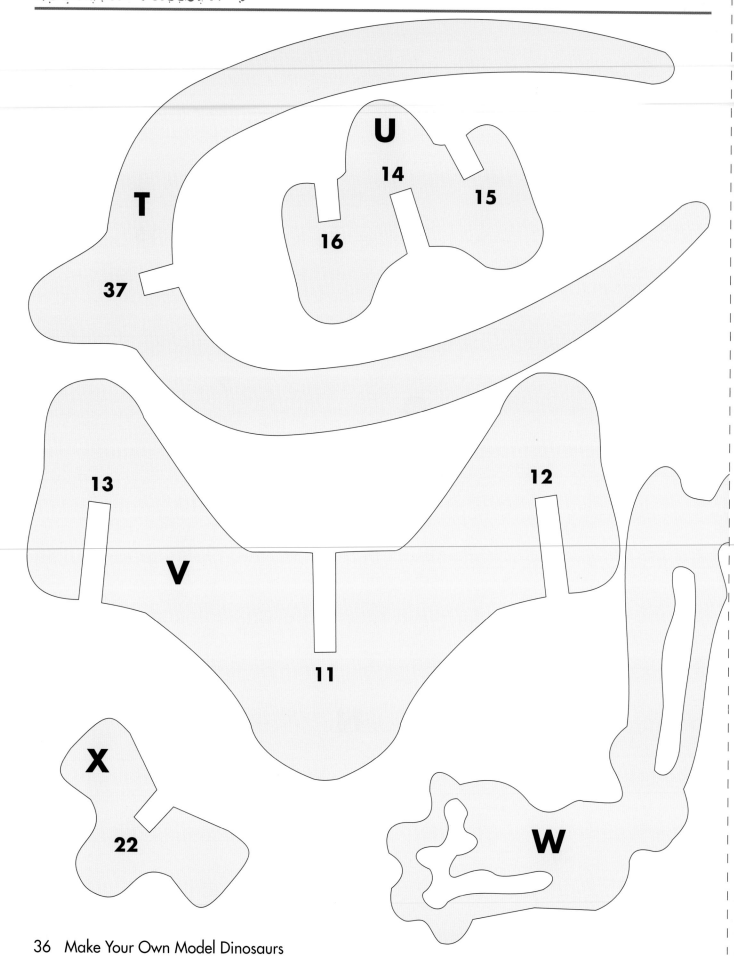

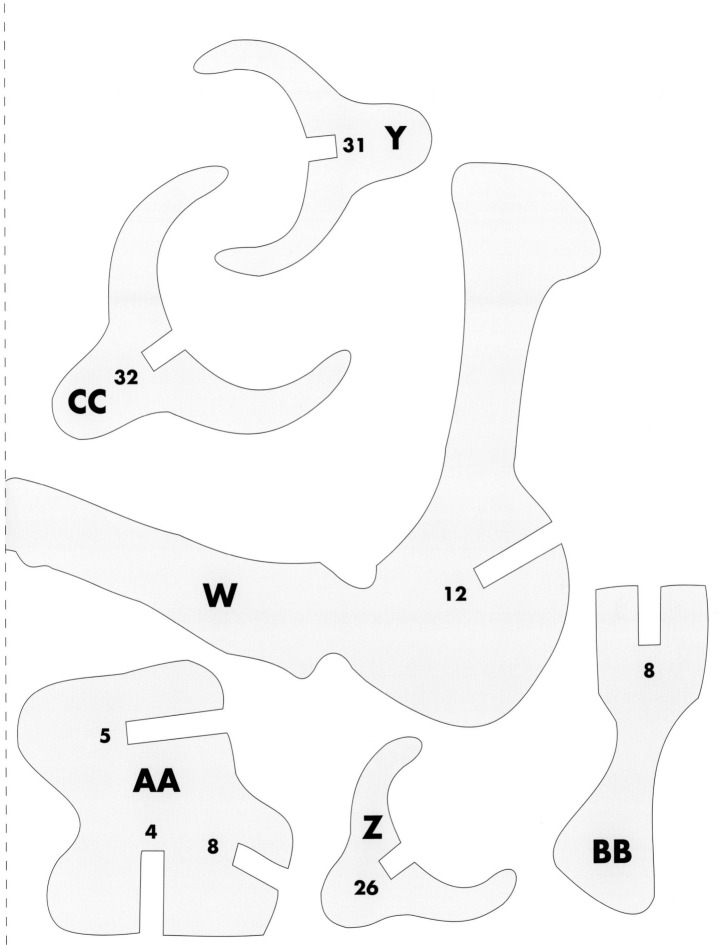

Y

31

CC 32

W

12

8

5

AA

4

8

Z

26

BB

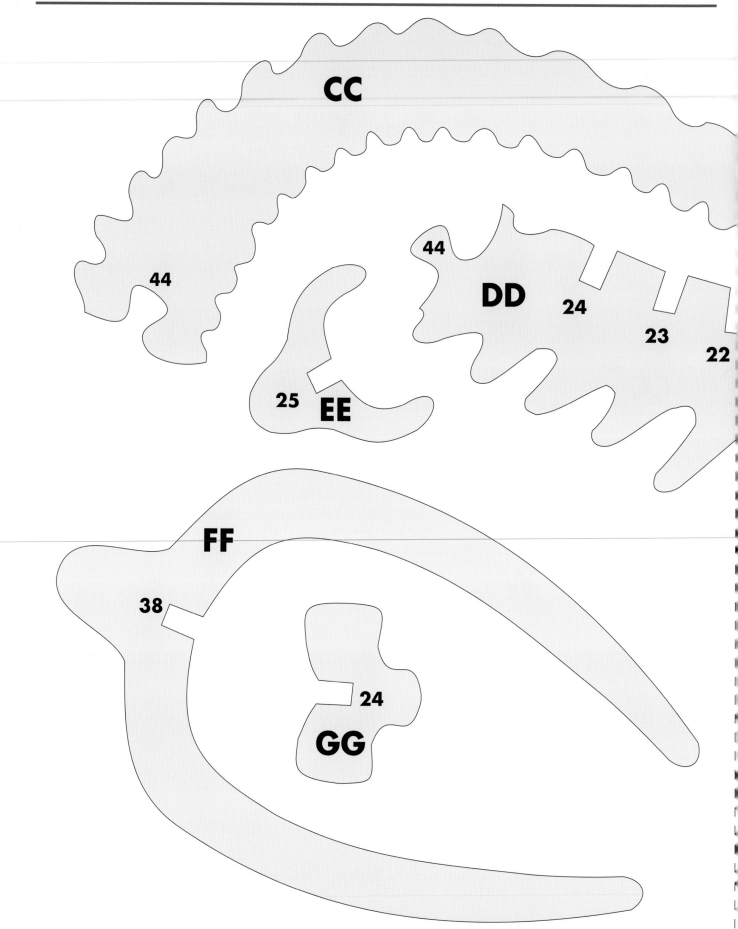

CC

44

44

DD

24

23

22

25 EE

FF

38

24

GG

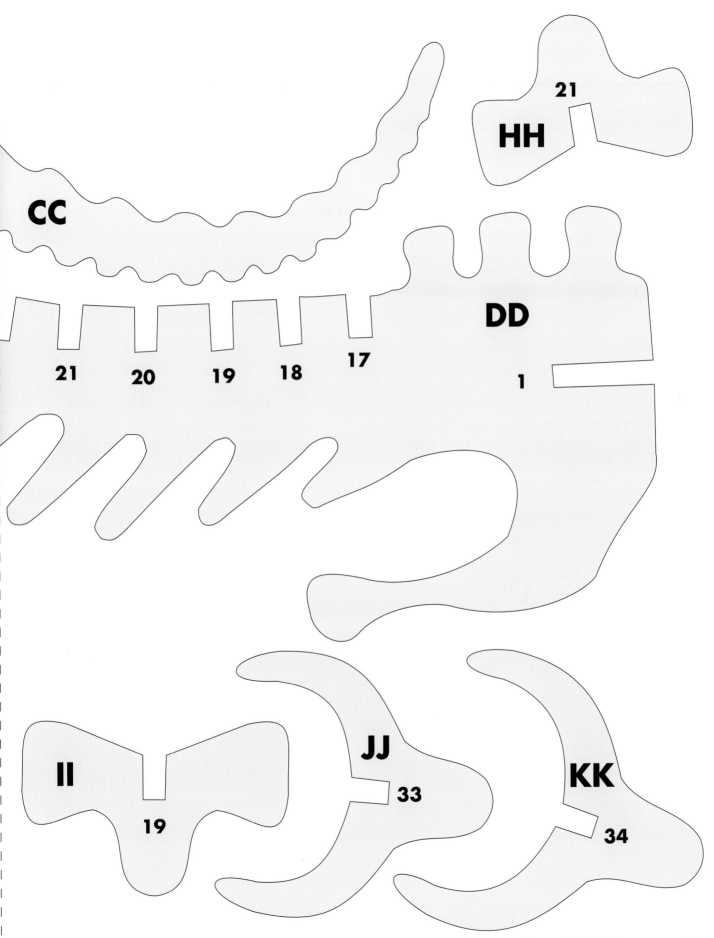

CC

HH
21

DD

21   20   19   18   17   1

II
19

JJ
33

KK
34

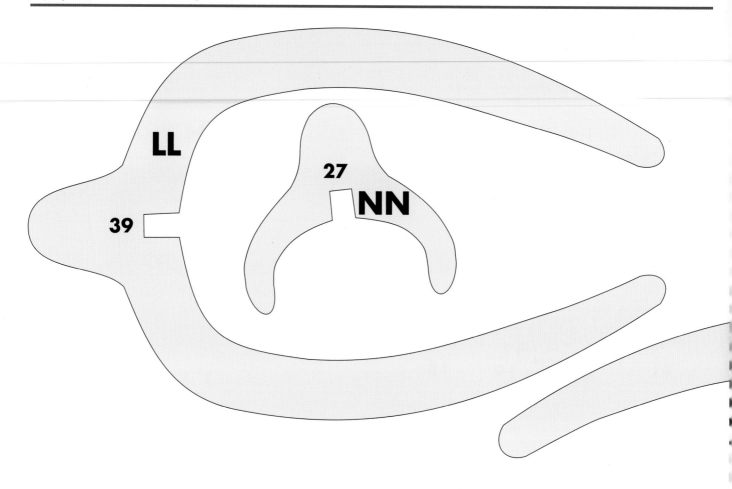

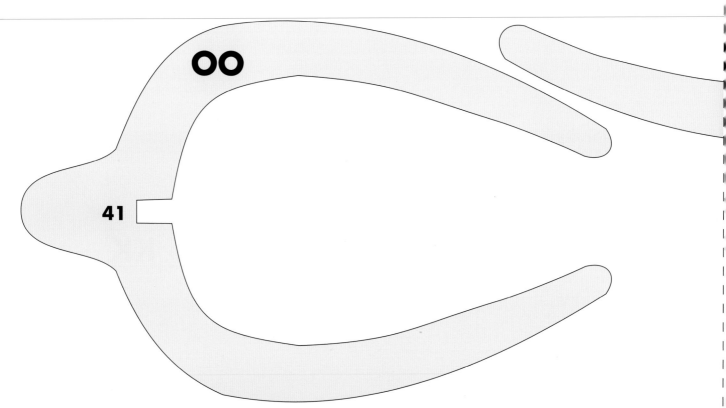

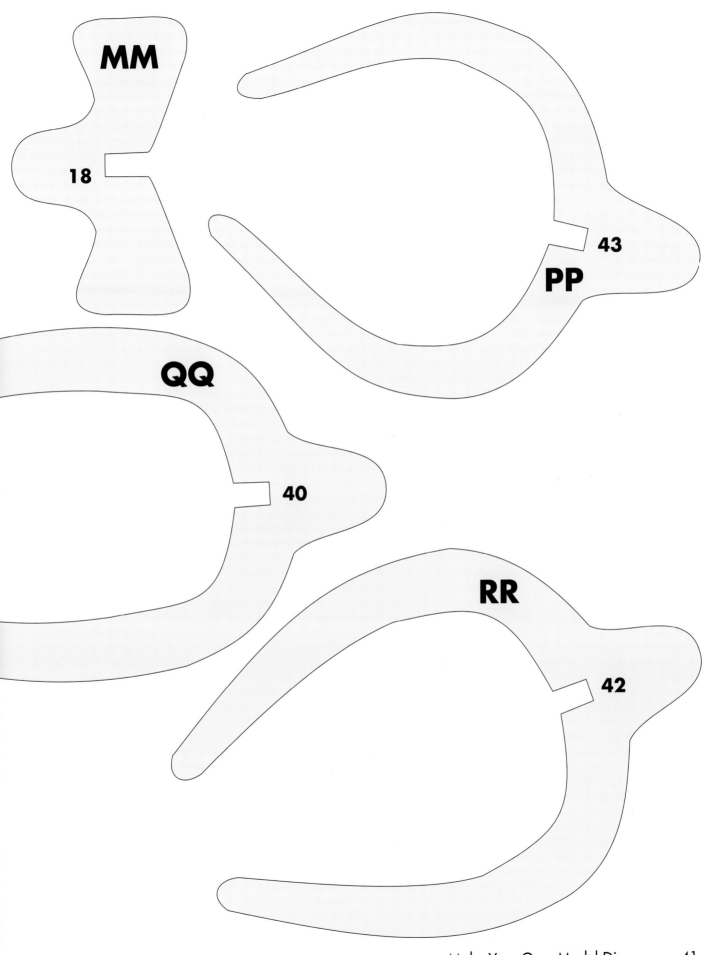

MM

18

PP

43

QQ

40

RR

42

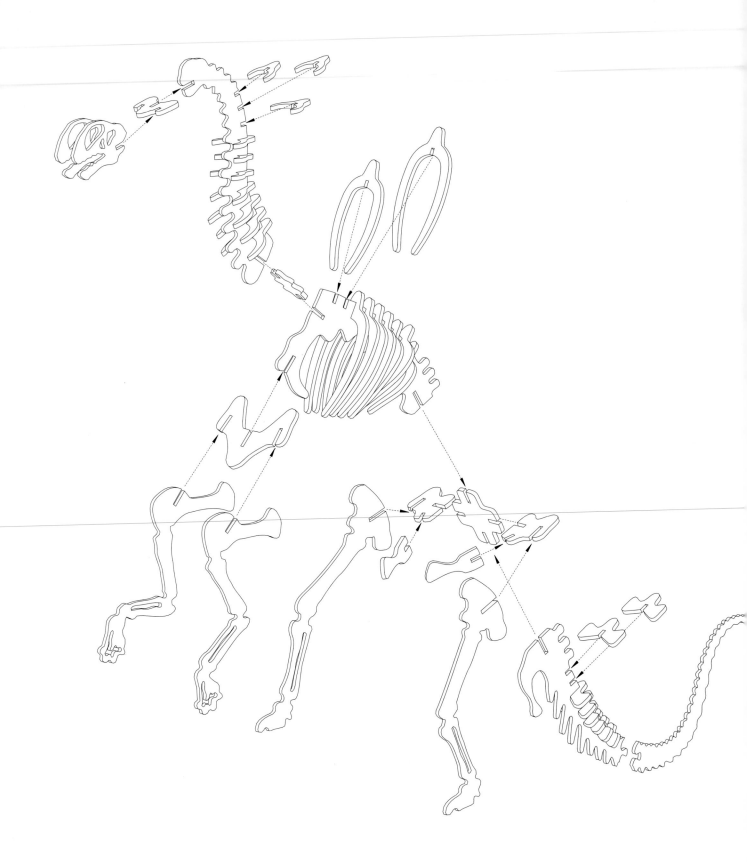

Pteranodon

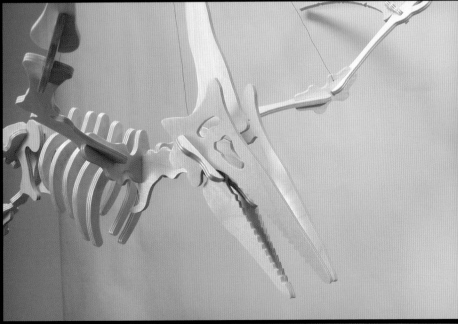

PTERANODON
(TER-an-oh-don)

- Flying lizard
- Name means "wing without tooth"
- Size: 23-foot wingspan
- Weight: 37 pounds
- Lived during the Cretaceous
- Bones first found in Wyoming in 1876

Pteranodon: Pattern 1

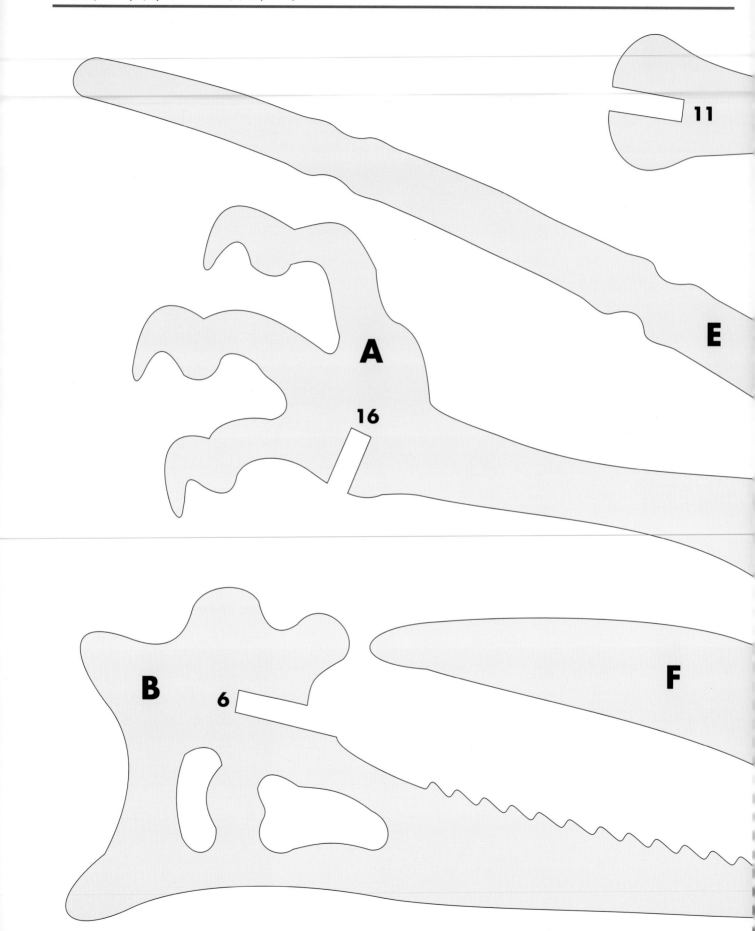

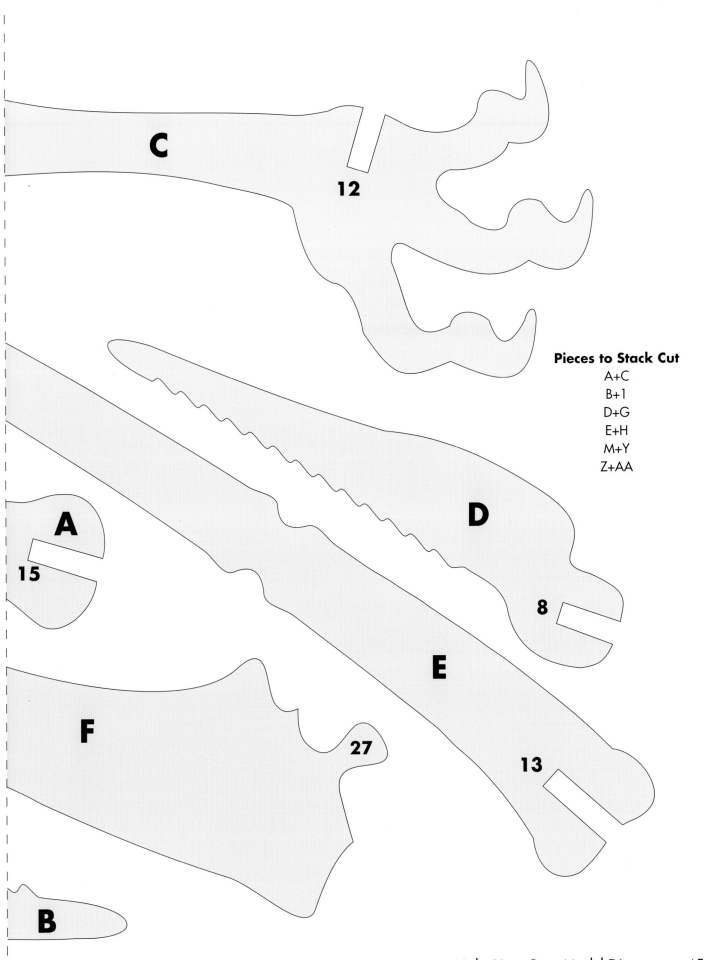

Pieces to Stack Cut
A+C
B+1
D+G
E+H
M+Y
Z+AA

C

12

A

15

D

8

E

F

27

13

B

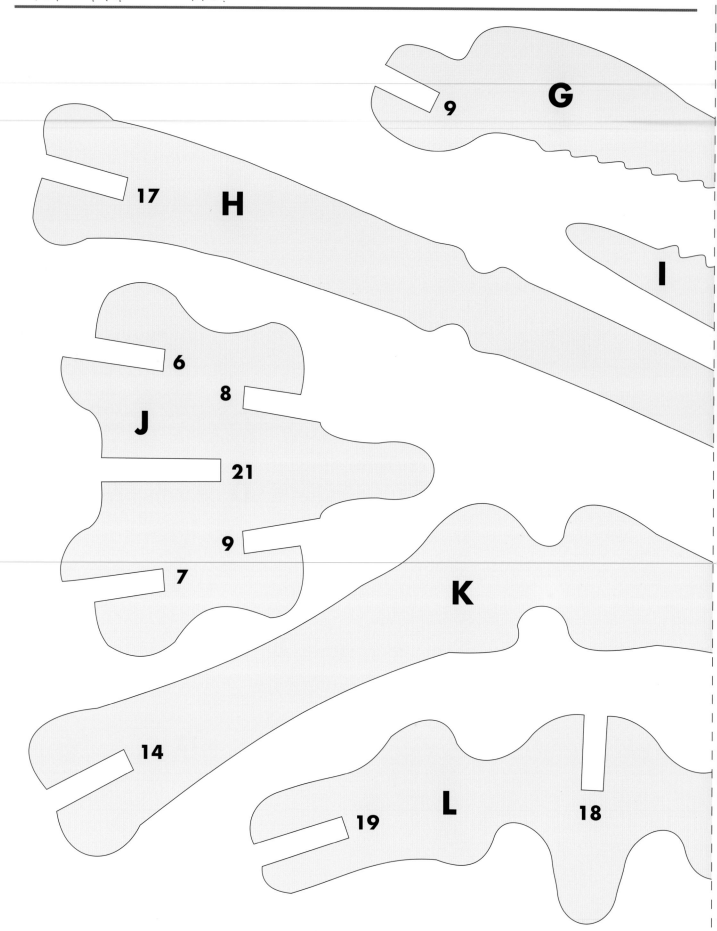

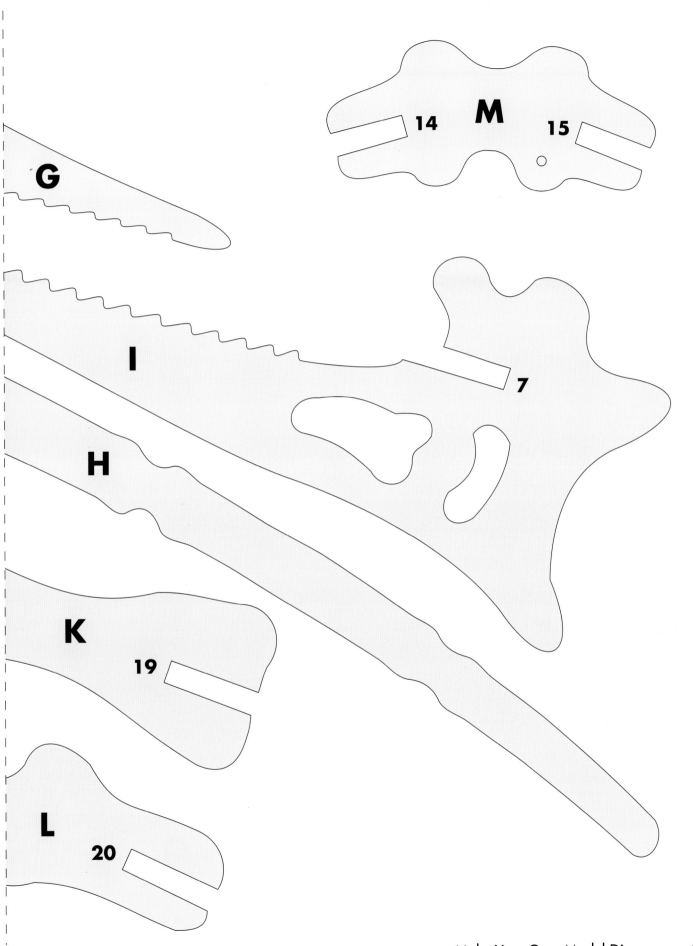

G

M
14
15

I

7

H

K
19

L
20

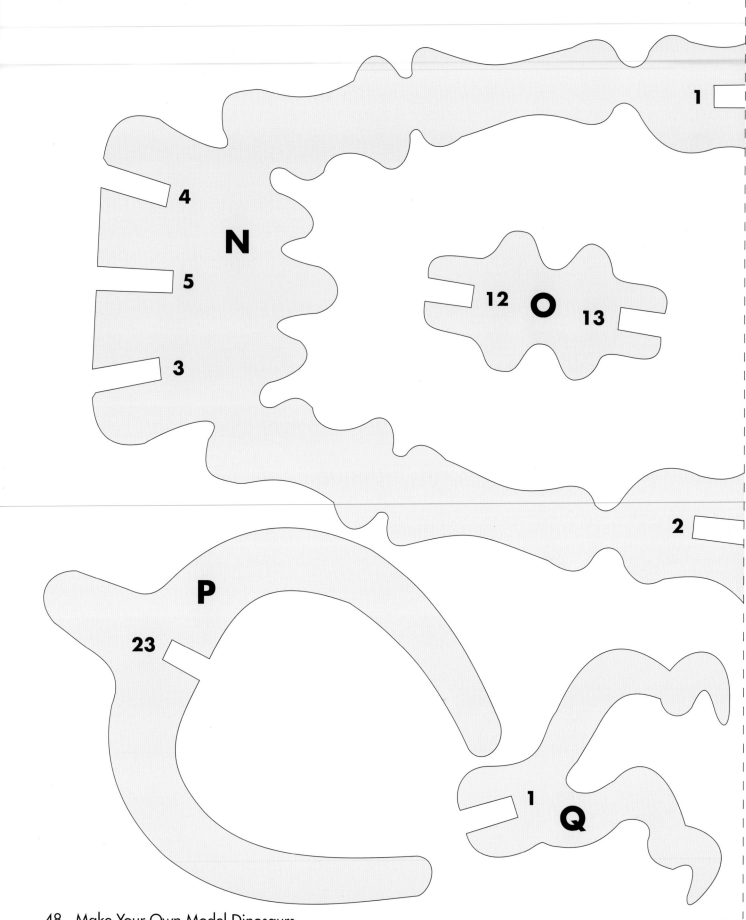

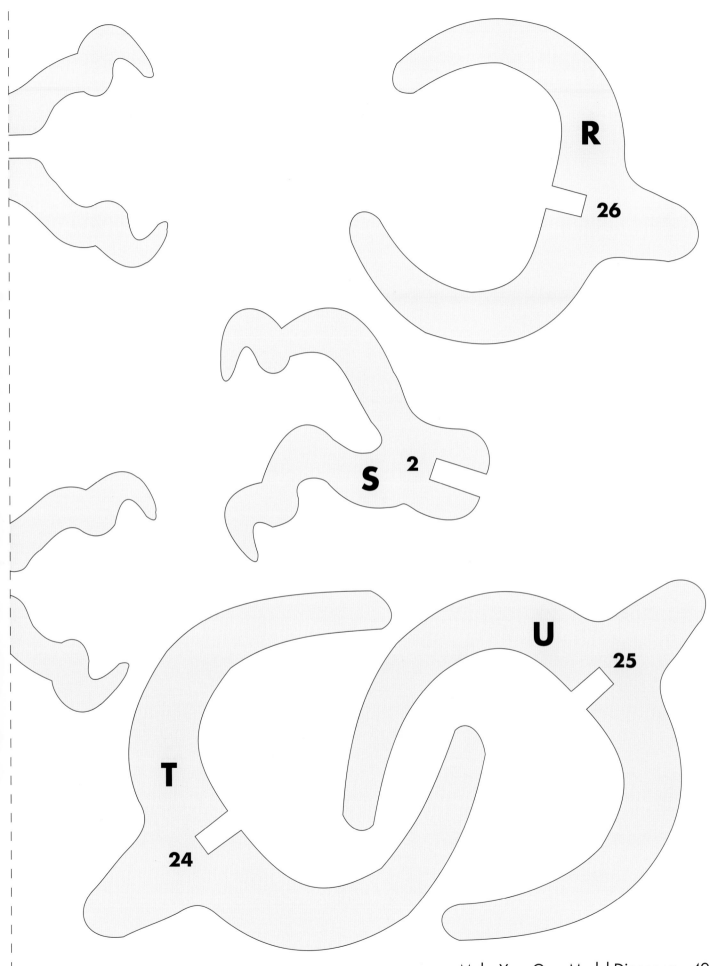

R

26

S   2

U

25

T

24

V

22

20

W

21 27

X

18   22   23   24

10   Y

11

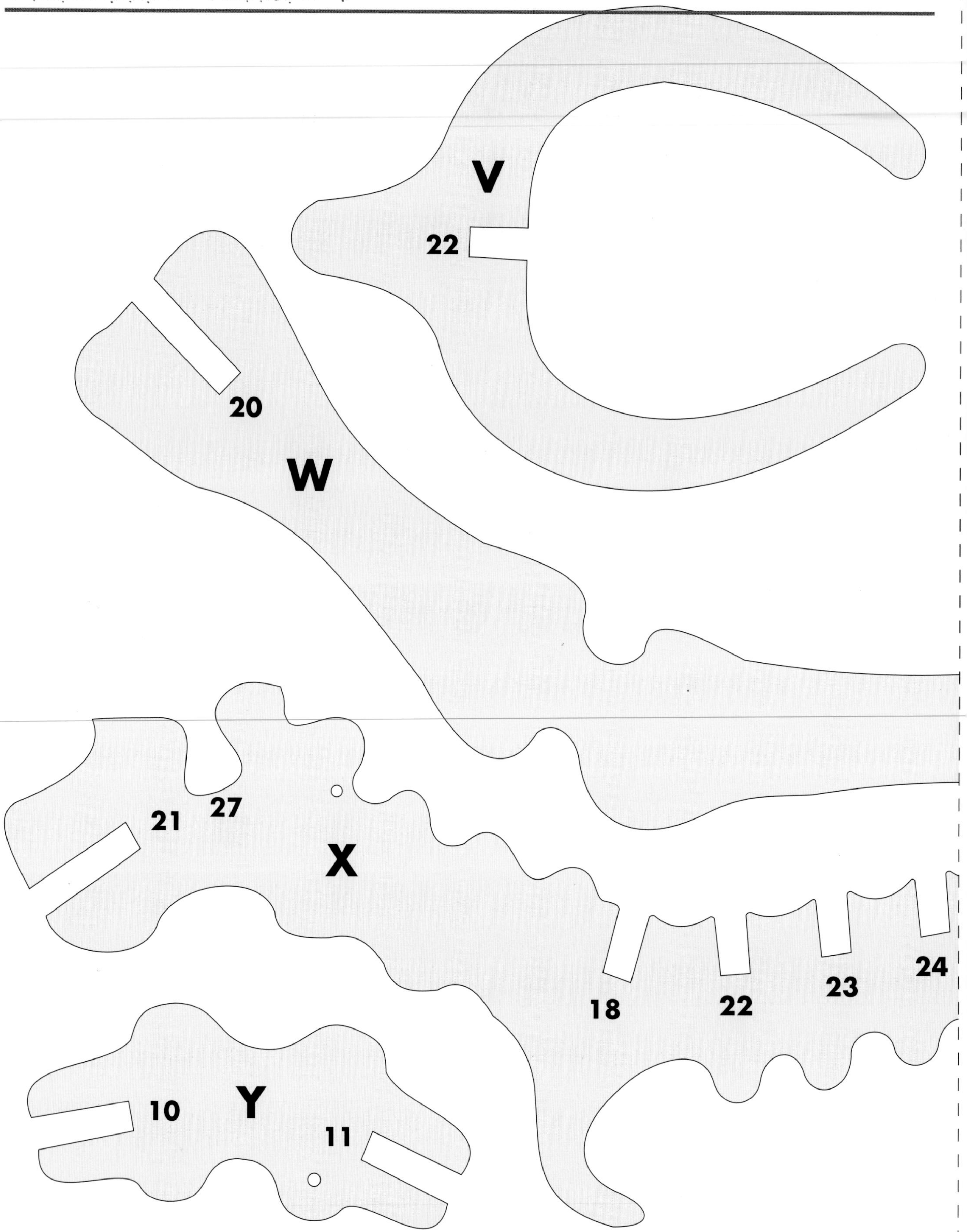

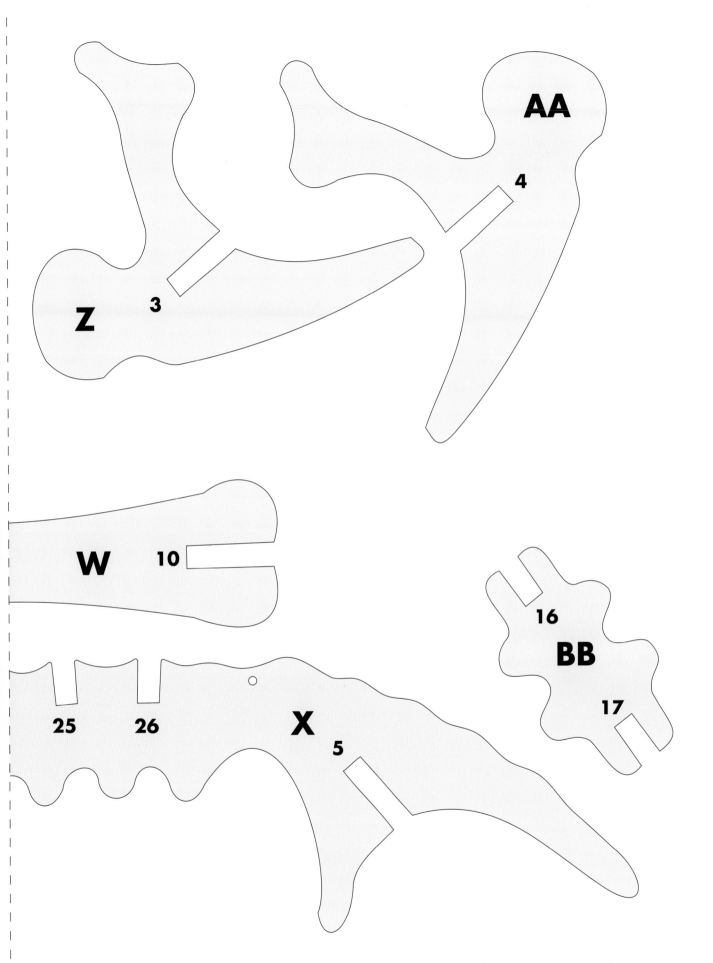

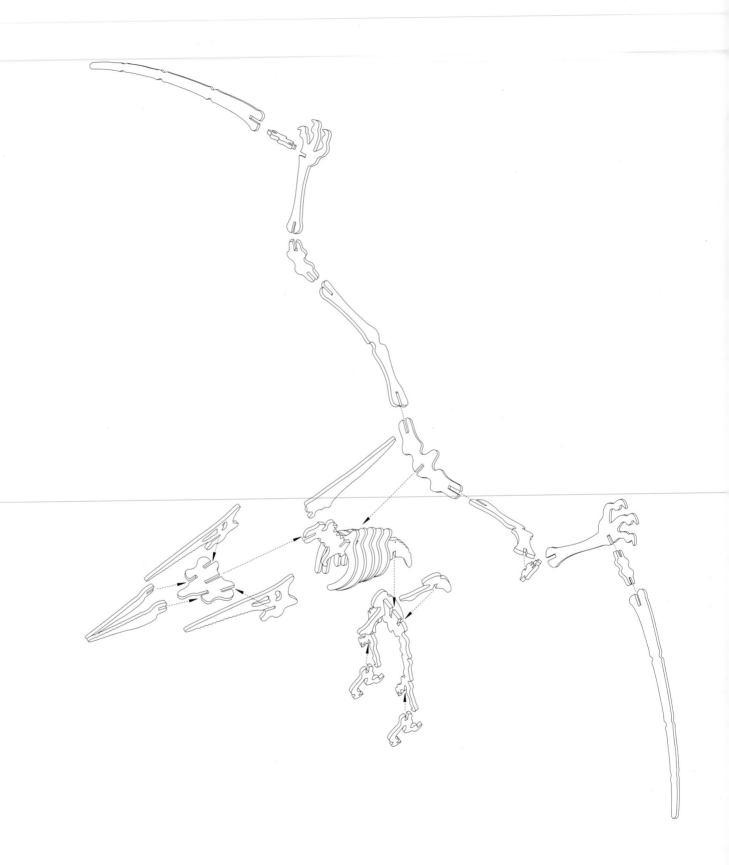

Spinosaurus

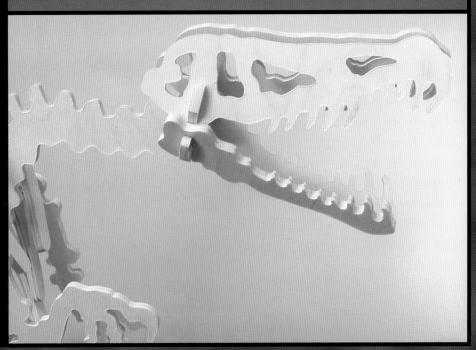

DINO FACTS

SPINOSAURUS
(SPYN-oh-sawr-us)

- Meat eater, biped
- Name means "spine lizard"
- Size: 14 feet tall,
  40 feet long
- Weight: 14,000 pounds
- Lived late in the Cretaceous
- Bones first found in Egypt

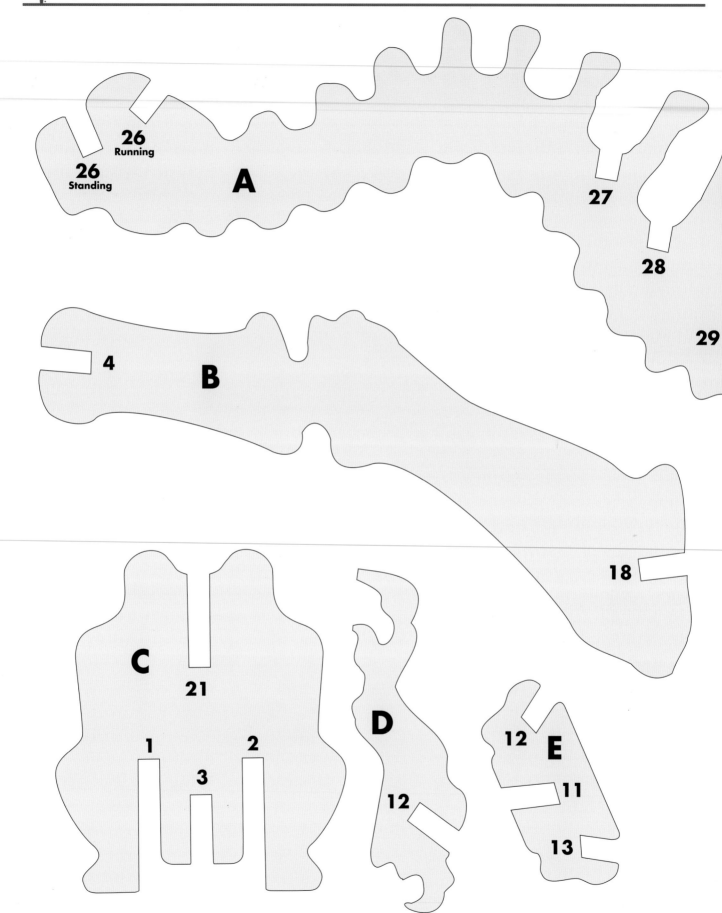

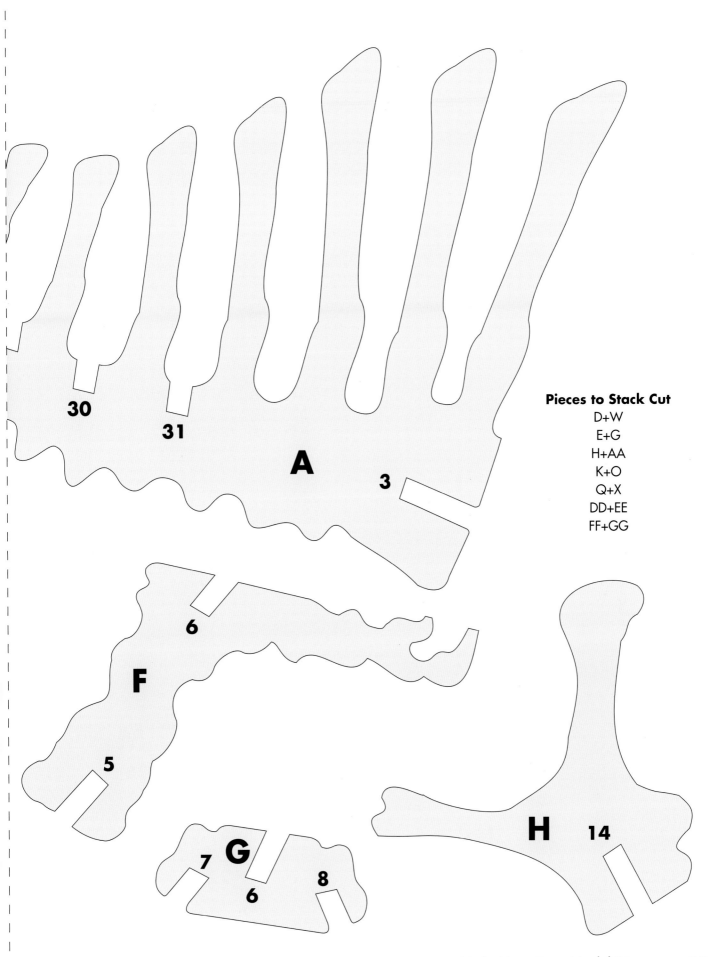

Pieces to Stack Cut
D+W
E+G
H+AA
K+O
Q+X
DD+EE
FF+GG

30

31

A

3

F

6

5

G

7

6

8

H 14

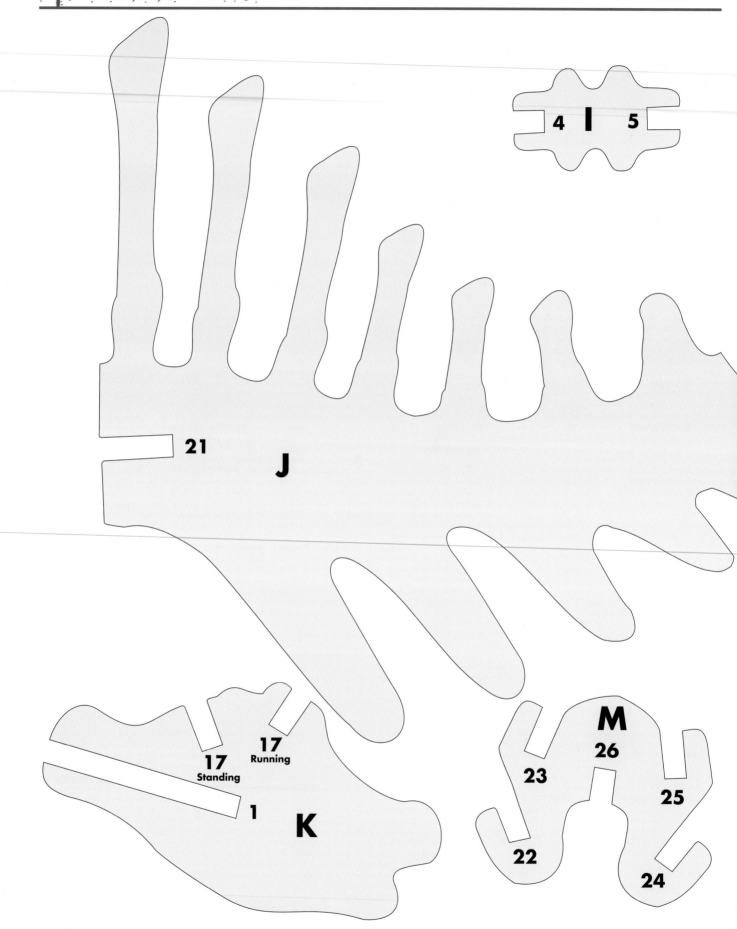

4 I 5

21

J

17
Running

17
Standing

1

K

M

26

23

22

25

24

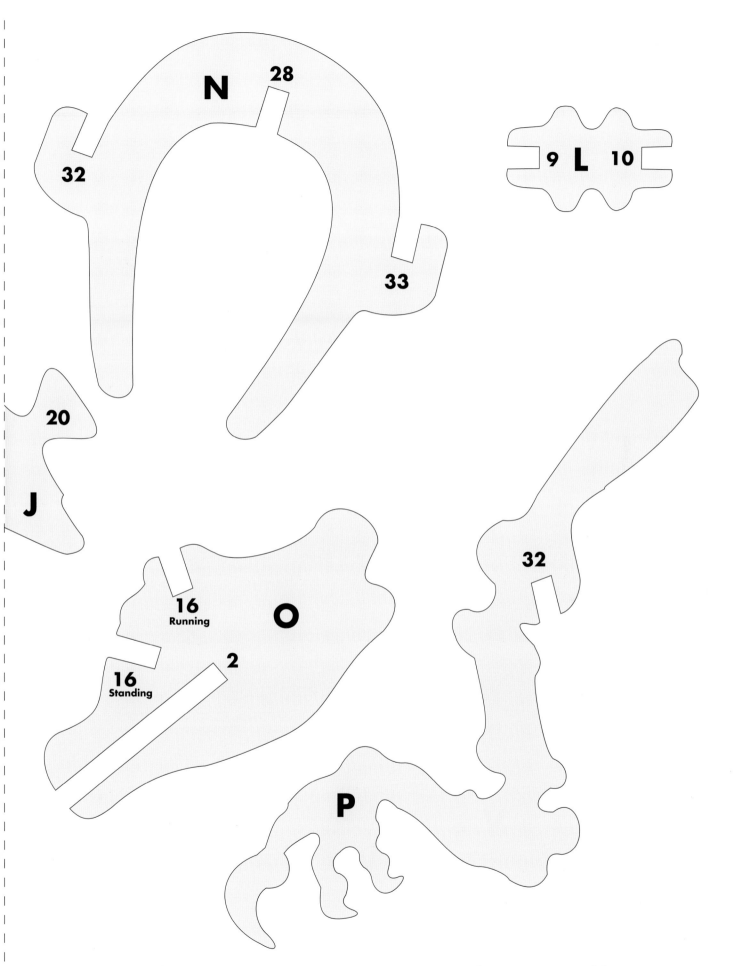

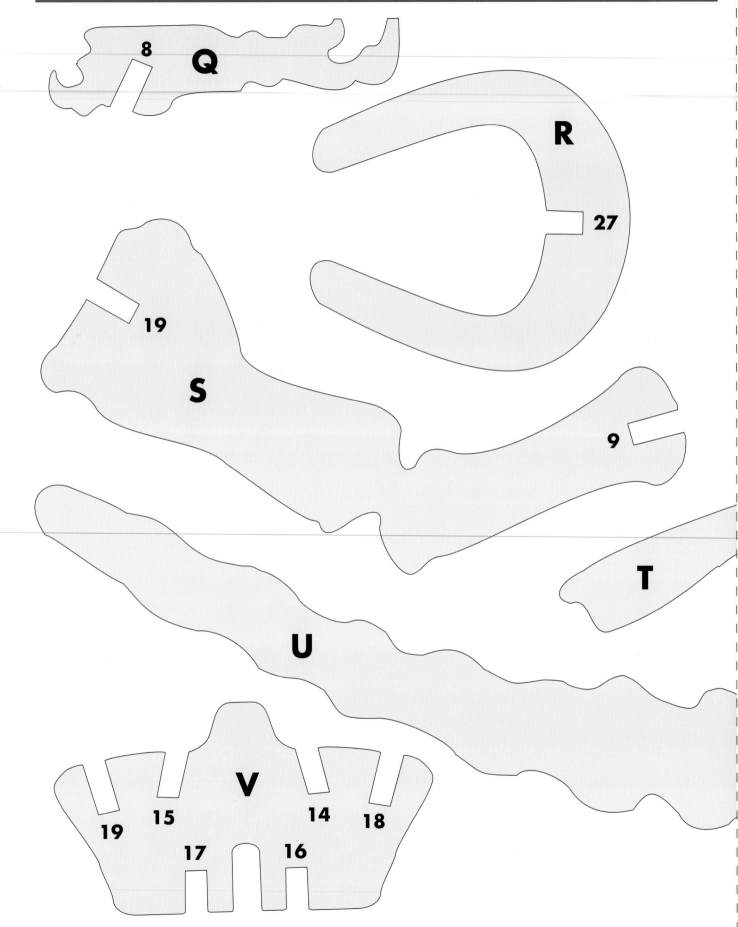

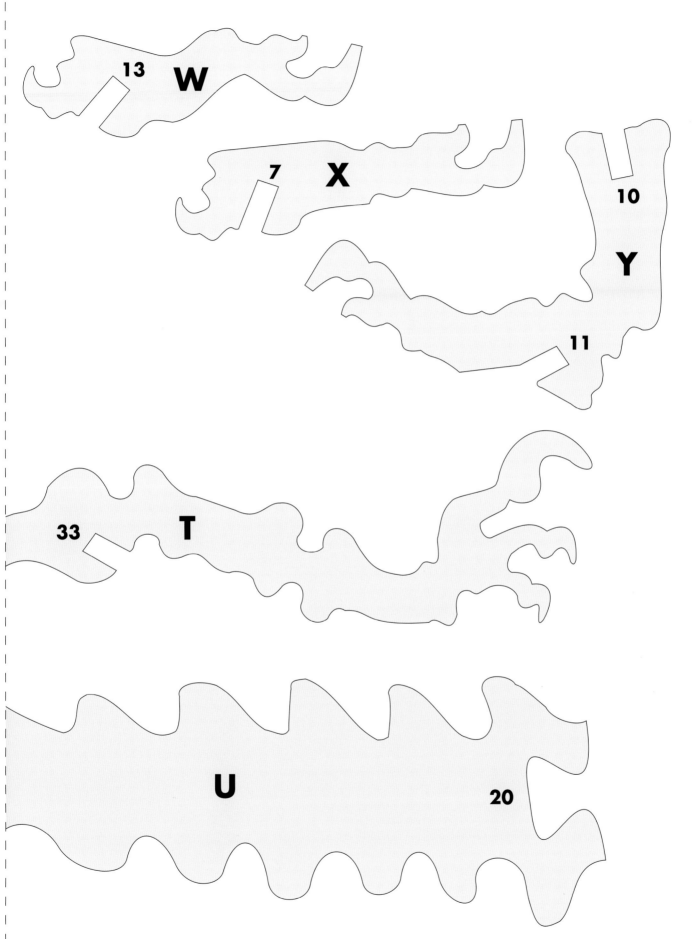

13 W

7 X

10

Y

11

33 T

U

20

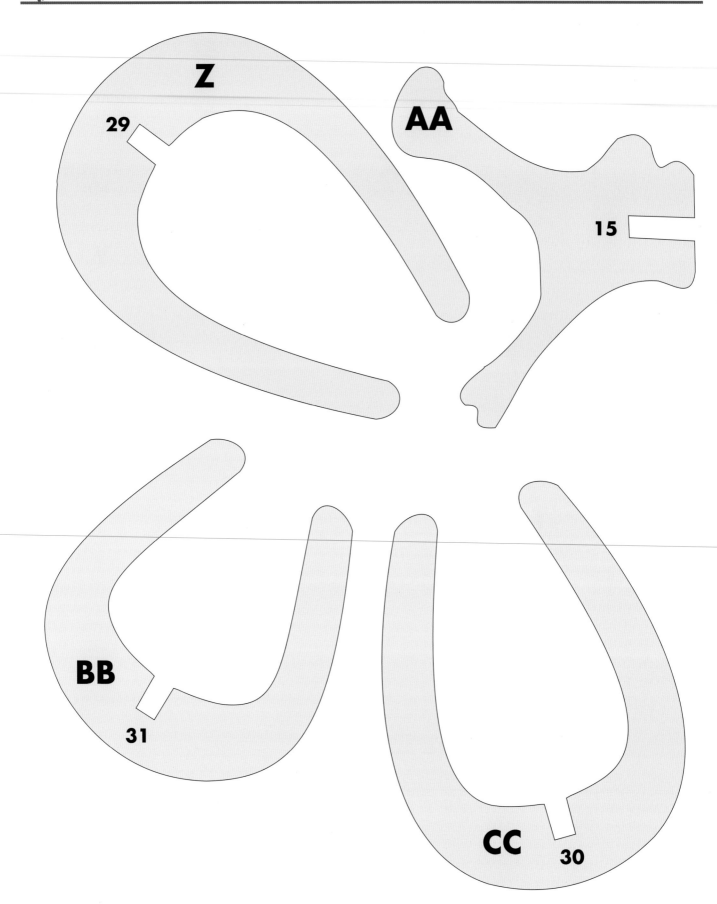

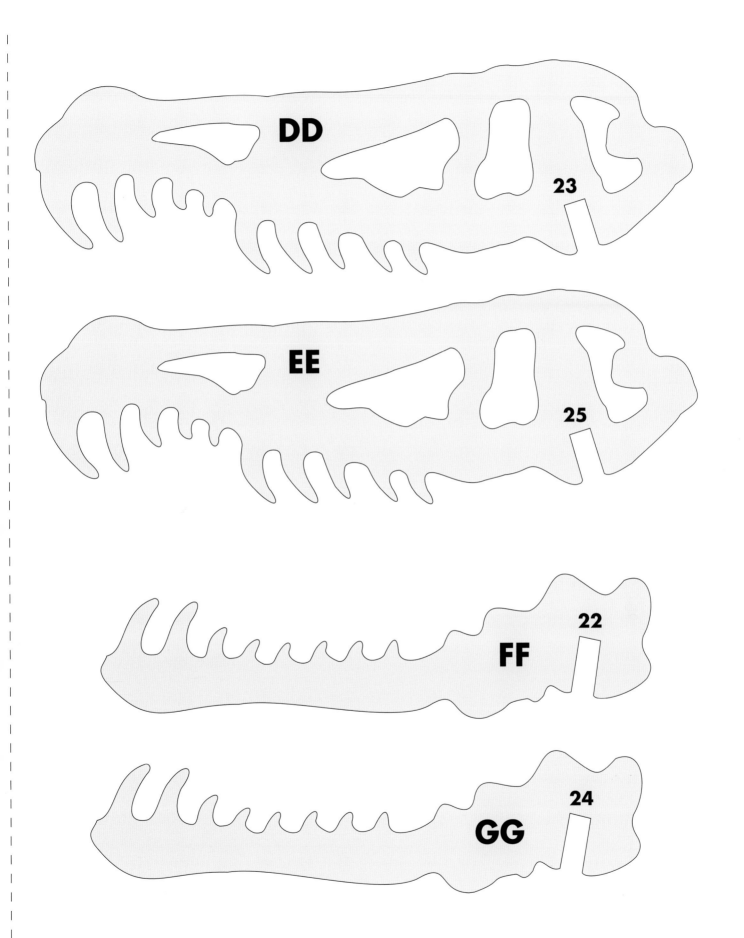

DD

23

EE

25

22

FF

24

GG

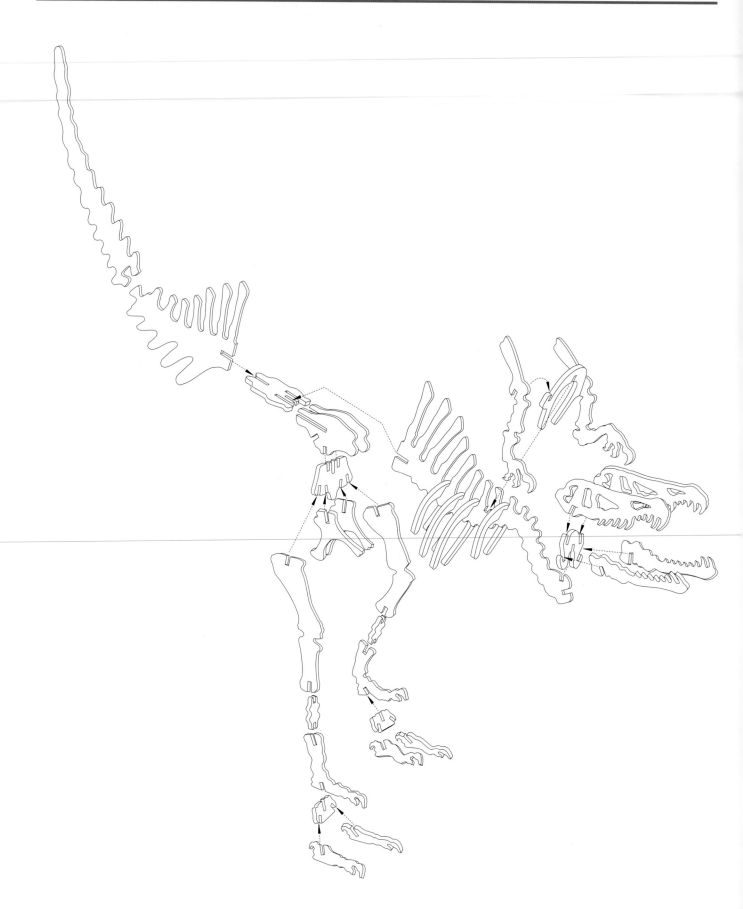

Stegosaurus

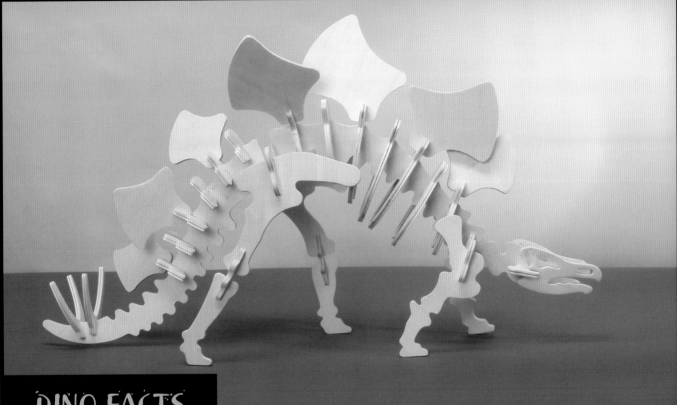

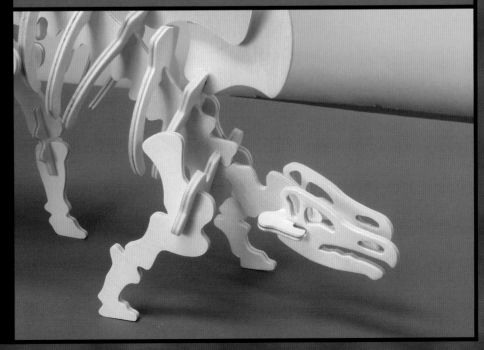

DINO FACTS

STEGOSAURUS
(STEG-oh-sawr-us)

- Plant eater, quadruped
- Name means "roof lizard"
- Size: 14 feet tall, 28 feet long
- Weight: 6,000 pounds
- Lived near the end of the Jurassic
- Bones found in western North America

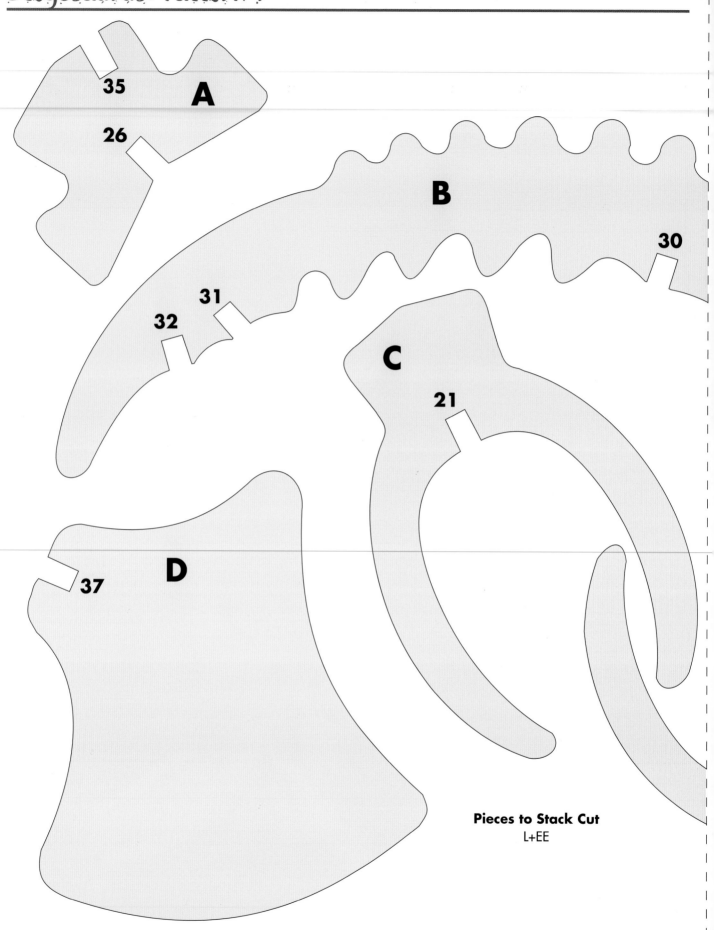

35

A

26

B

30

31

32

C

21

D

37

Pieces to Stack Cut
L+EE

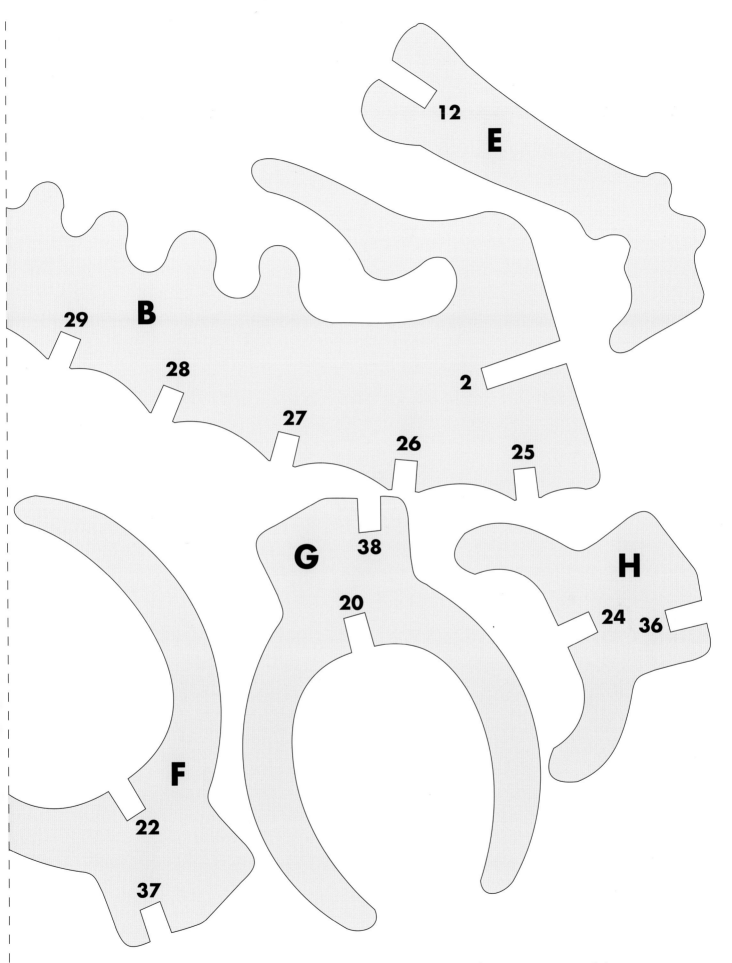

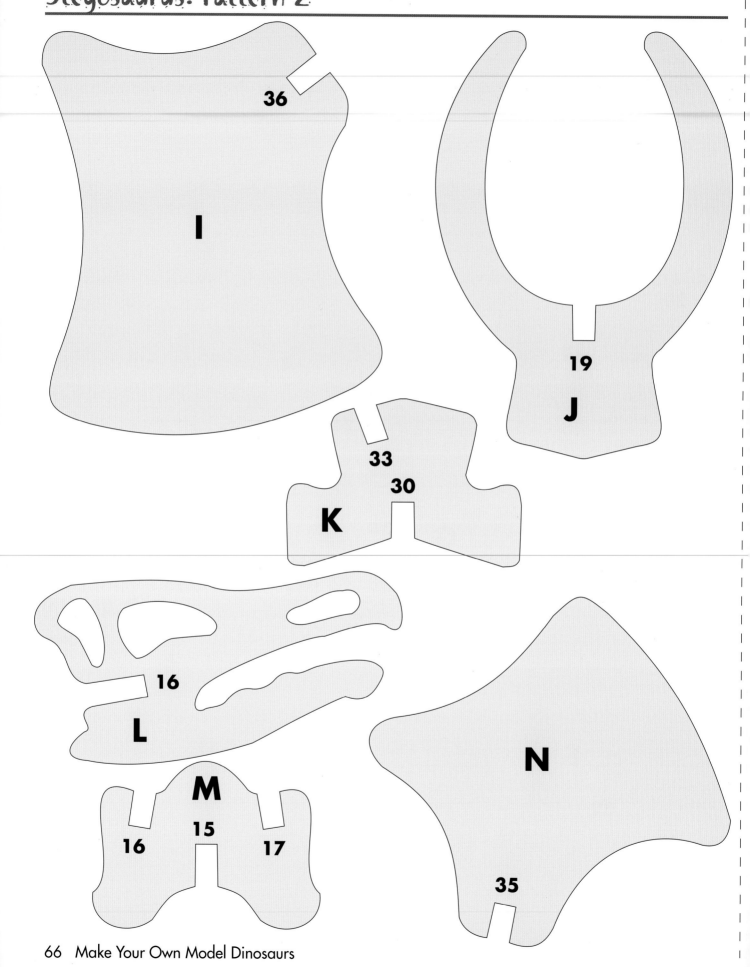

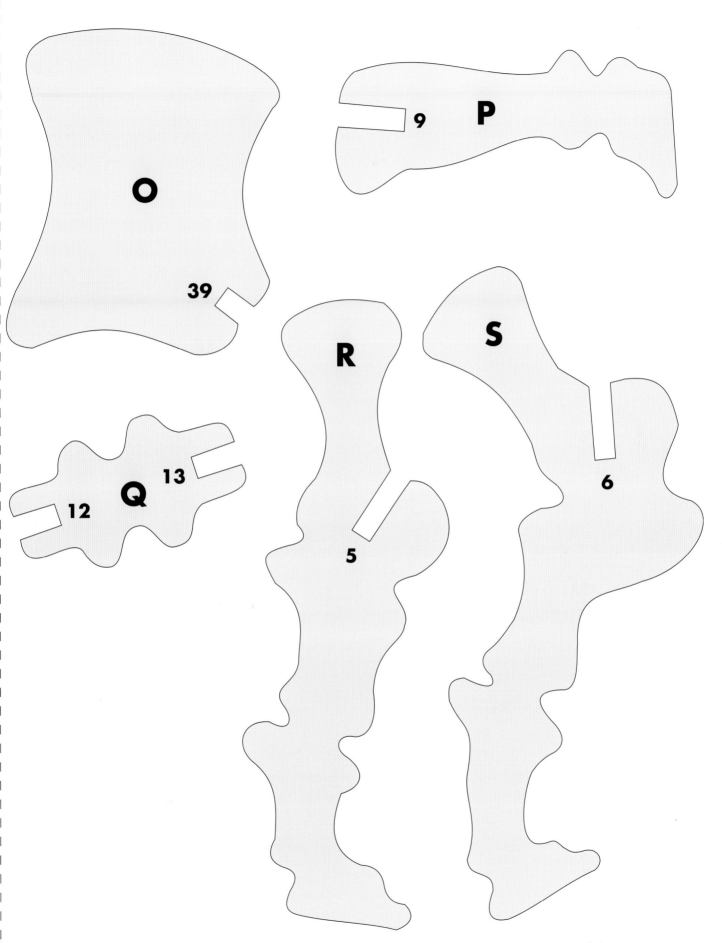

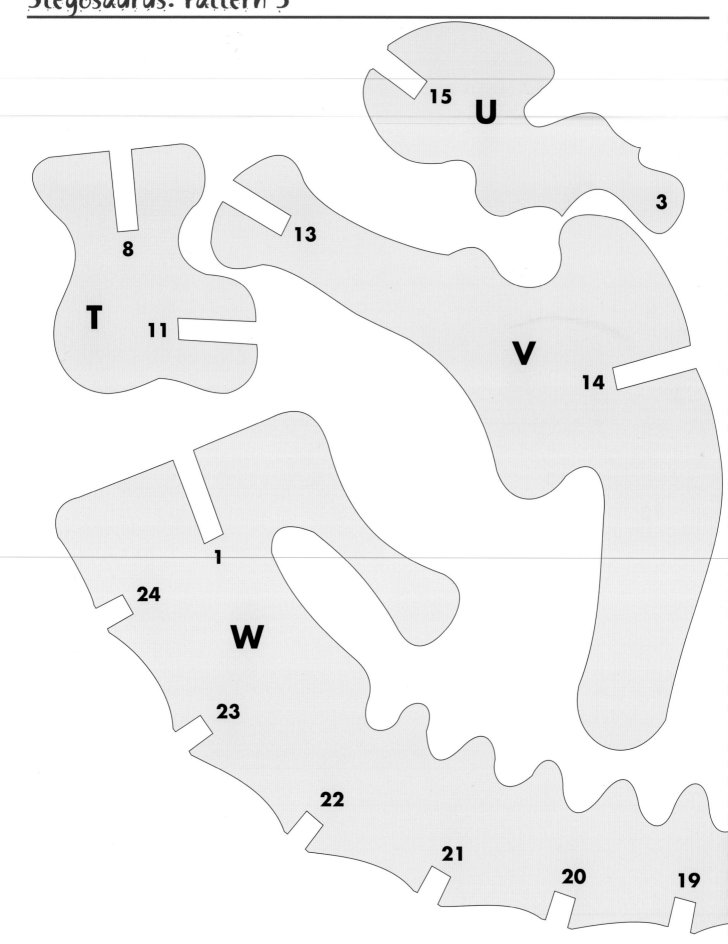

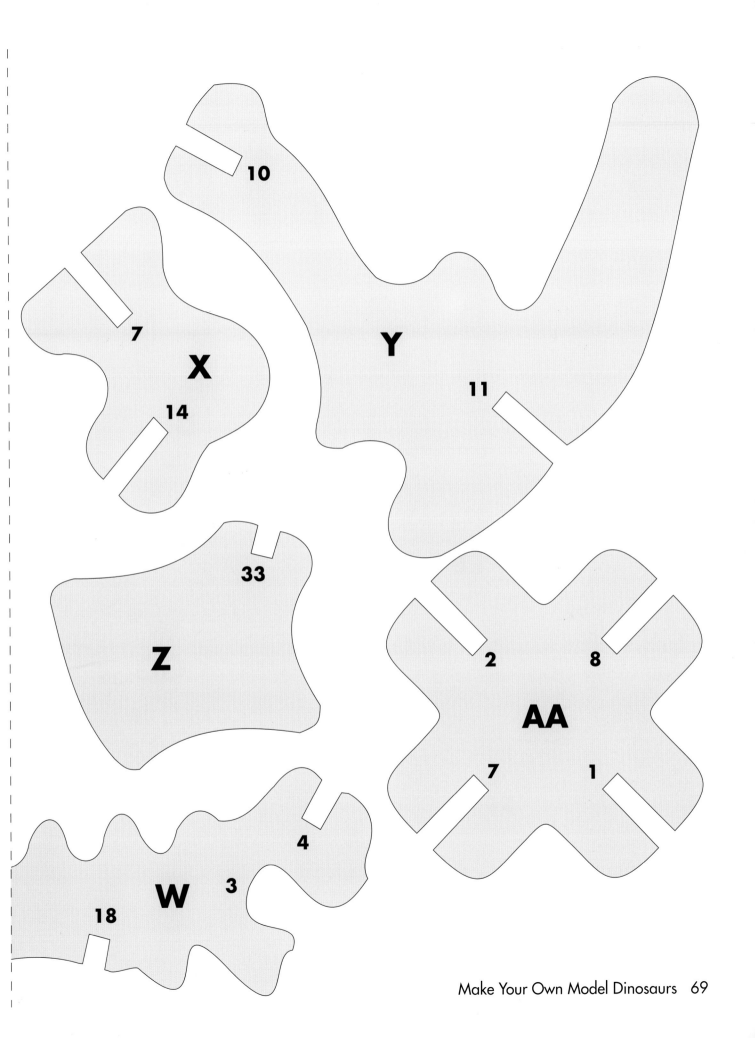

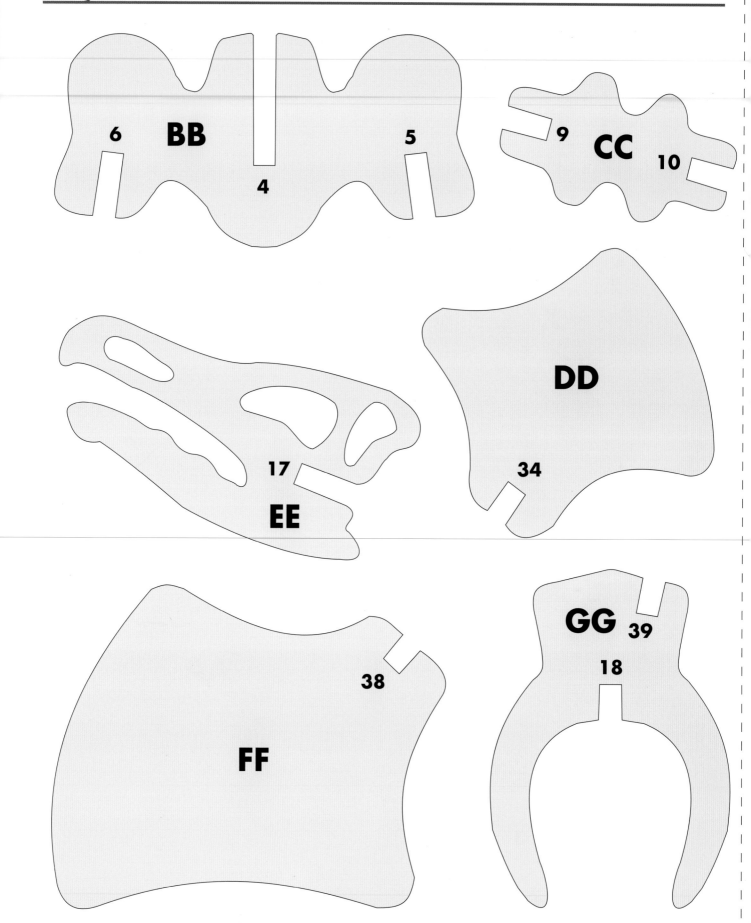

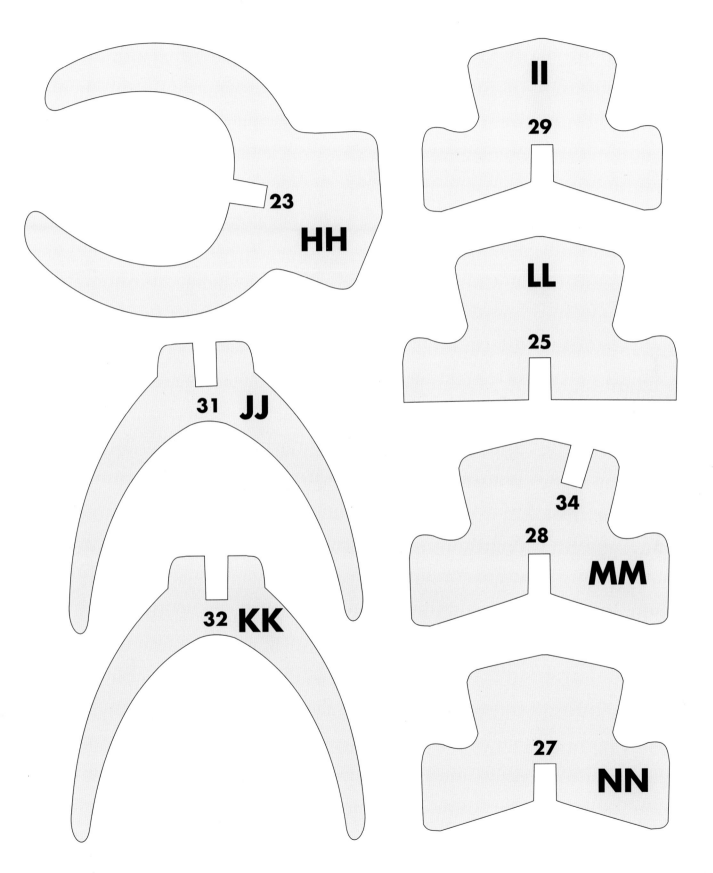

II
29

LL
25

23
HH

31 JJ

34
28
MM

32 KK

27
NN

Velociraptor

DINO FACTS

VELOCIRAPTOR
(Vu-LA-si-rap-tur)

- Meat eater, biped
- Name means "quick plunderer" or "rapid robber"
- Size: 2.5 feet tall, 5.9 feet long
- Weight: 200 pounds
- Lived during the Upper Cretaceous
- Bones found in Mongolia, China and Russia

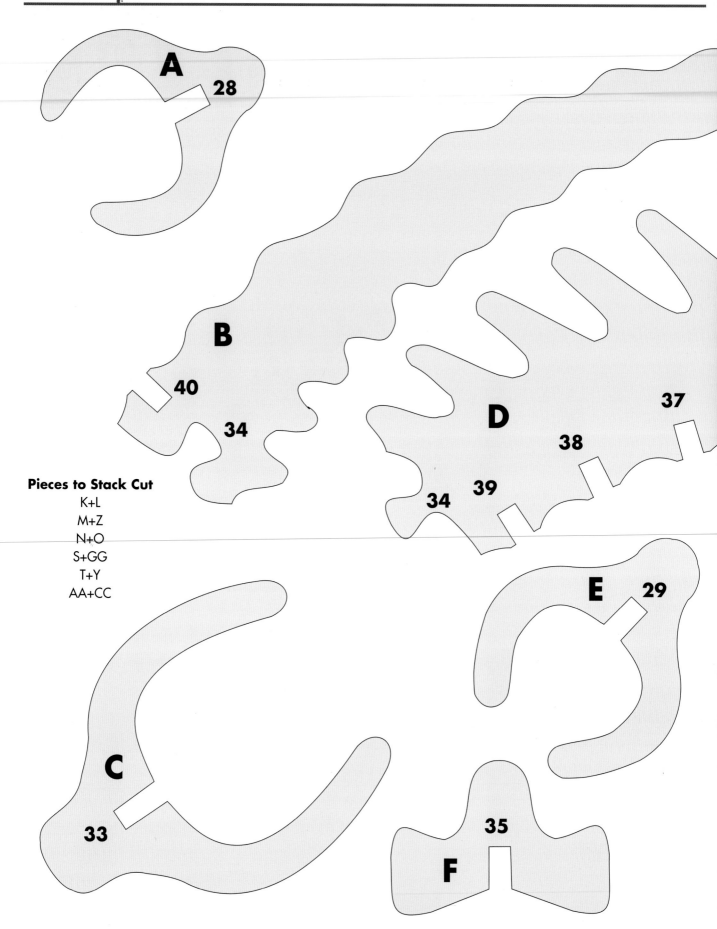

A 28

B

40

34

D

37

38

34 39

Pieces to Stack Cut
K+L
M+Z
N+O
S+GG
T+Y
AA+CC

E 29

C

33

F 35

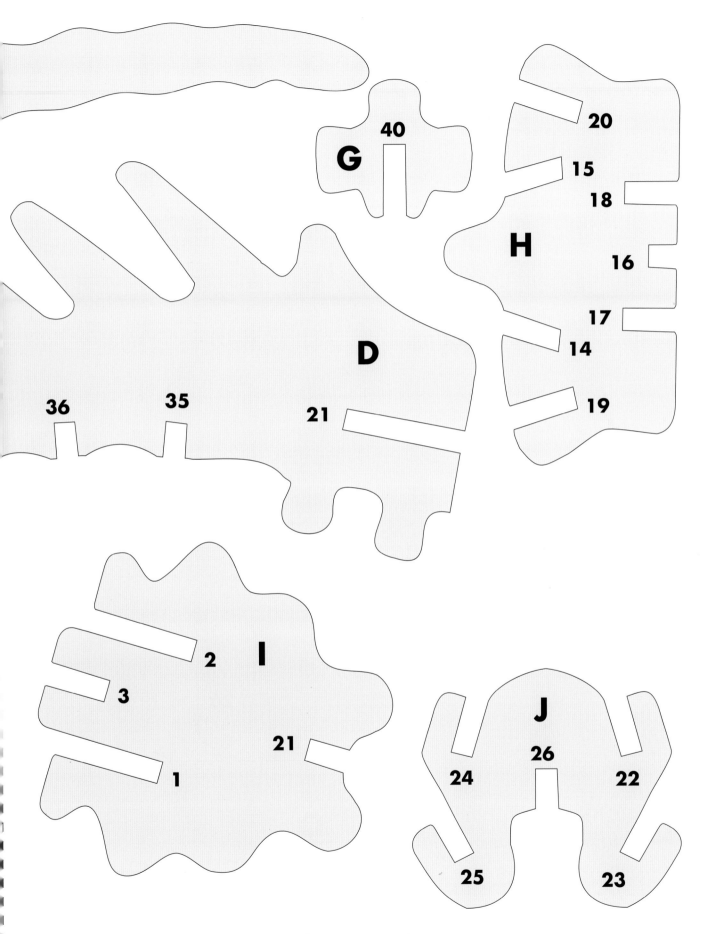

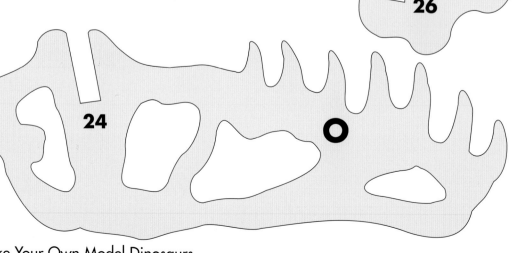

K
7

L
8

M
12

N
22

P
26

24
O

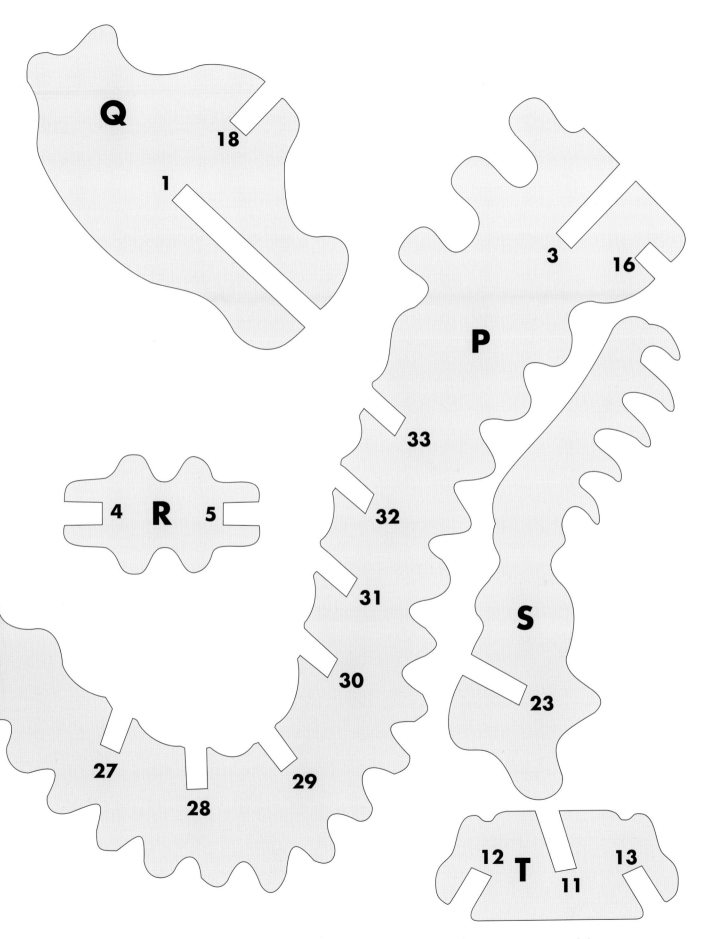

Velociraptor: Pattern 3

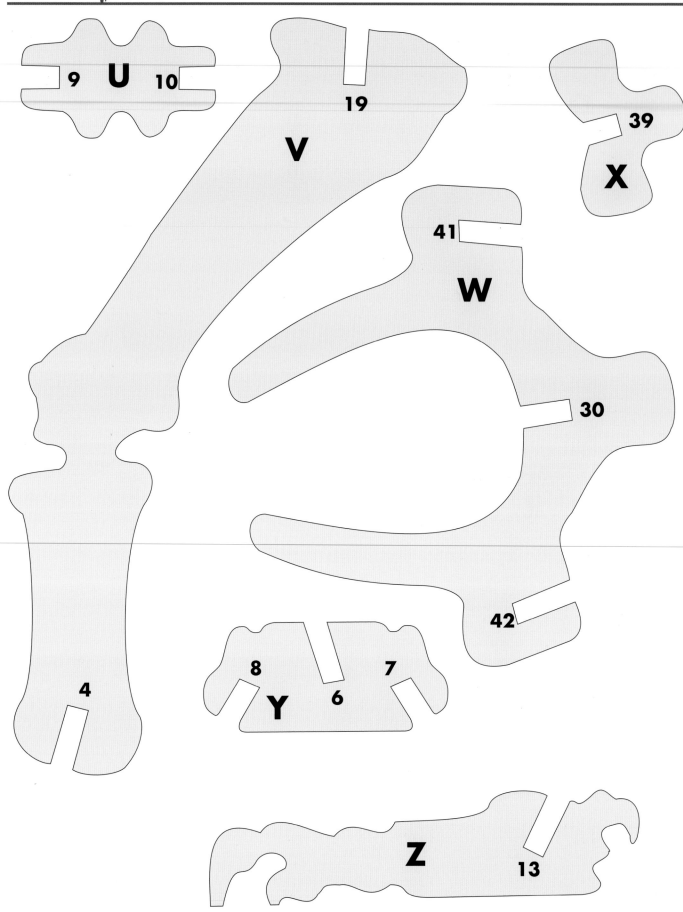

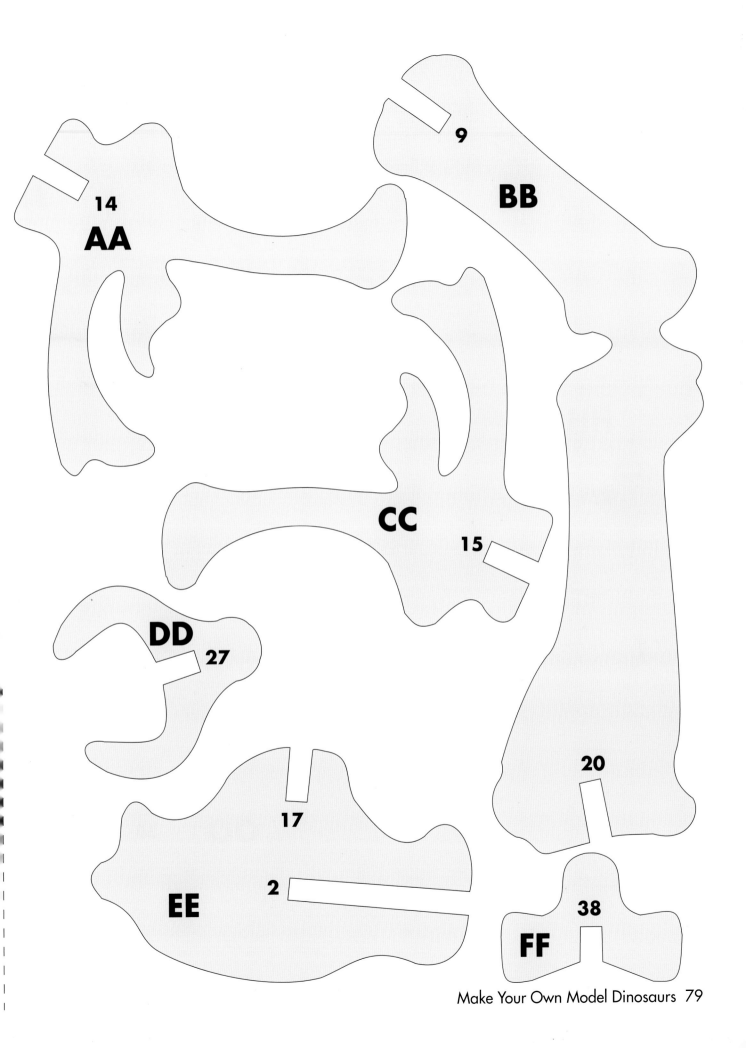

14

AA

9

BB

CC

15

DD

27

17

20

2

EE

38

FF

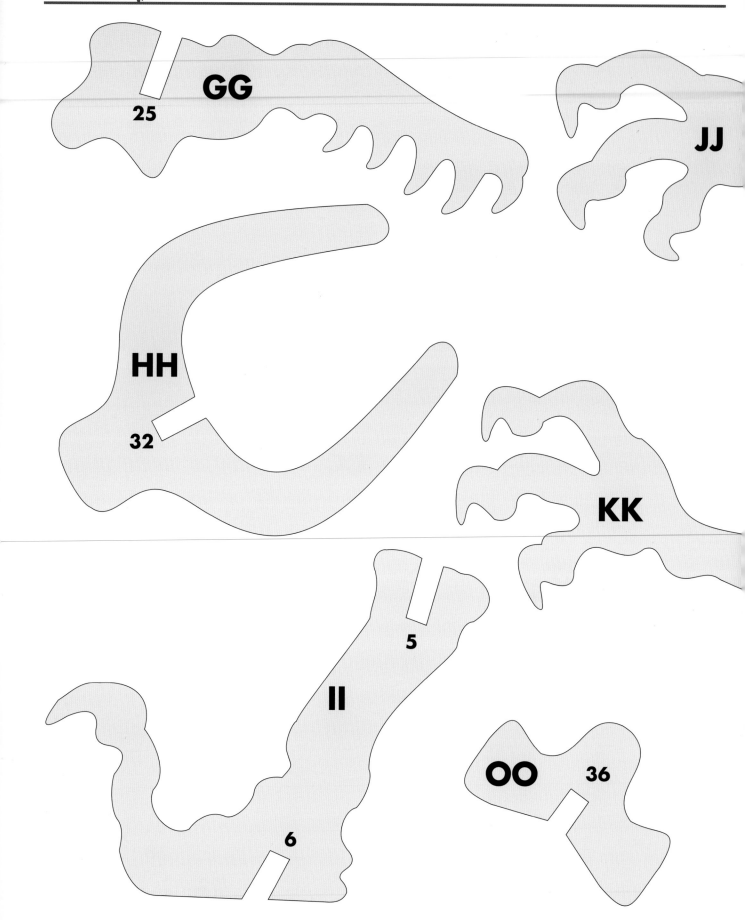

GG

25

JJ

HH

32

KK

5

II

OO   36

6

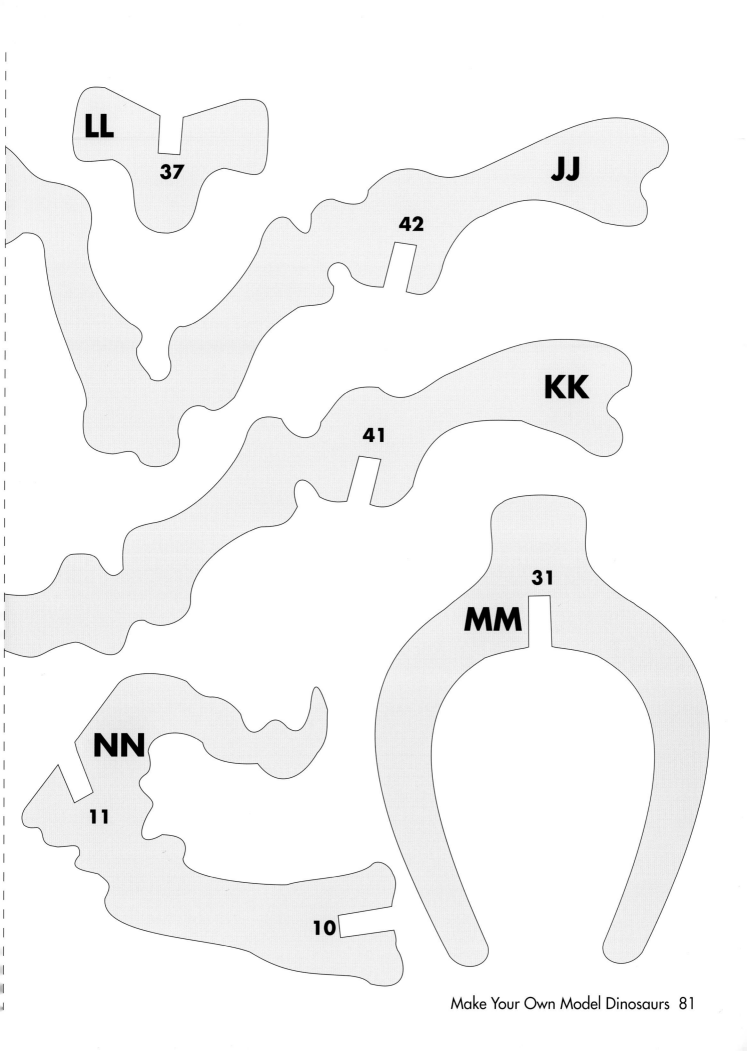

LL

37

JJ

42

KK

41

31

MM

NN

11

10

Velociraptor: Assembly Drawing

More Great Project Books from Fox Chapel Publishing

Wooden Chess Sets You Can Make
By Diana Thompson
Handcraft a classic or contemporary chess set that will be cherished for years to come. You will learn to create each piece by using compound cuts on the scroll saw. Patterns and full-color photographs for each of the playing pieces (king, queen, bishop, knight, rook, and pawn) are included. Instructions and pattern for a beautiful inlay playing board also included.
ISBN: 1-56523-188-0, 72 pages, soft cover, $14.95.

Making Toys
By Sam Martin and Roger Schroeder
The most complete book on making collectable toys from wood! Features step-by-step instructions, full measured drawings, and plans to build a Peterbild 1932 Buick Sedan, Ford Model A Pick-up, Van and Flat Bed Trailer.
ISBN: 1-56523-079-5, 103 pages, soft cover, $17.95

Making Lawn Ornaments in Wood
By Paul Meisel
Stop traffic with these popular lawn and garden accessories. Features complete instructions and patterns for thirty-four projects, a full-color gallery, and a "how-to" paint mixing chart. Detailed instructions cover choosing the wood, transferring, cutting & painting. Includes over 20 ready to use full-size patterns.
ISBN: 1-56523- 163-5, 72 pages, soft cover, $14.95

Fireplace and Mantel Ideas, 2nd edition
By John Lewman
Design, build and install your dream fireplace mantel with this updated edition of a popular classic. Inside you'll find two new step-by-steps on carving a rustic mantel with woodcarving tools and building a classic fireplace mantel using general woodworking skills and tools. In addition, the author includes an amazing selection of classic fireplace mantel designs including English traditional, Country French, Victorian, Art Nouveau, and more.
ISBN: 1-56523-229-1, 196 pages, soft cover, $19.95

Scroll Saw Toys & Vehicles
By Stan Graves
Make durable wooden toys that will bring smiles to children of any age. The book features sturdy, practical designs, ready-to-use patterns for ten vehicles, and full-color photographs of the finished projects.
ISBN: 1-56523-115-5, 48 pages, soft cover, $15.95

Making Construction Vehicles for Kids
By Luc St-Amour
Capture a child's imagination with any of these eight toys. Includes parts lists, full-size cutting templates and step-by-step drawings for completing 8 construction vehicles — with moving parts — for children.
ISBN: 1-56523-151-1, 116 pages, soft cover, $15.95

Realistic Construction Models You Can Make
By Luc St-Amour
Make eight display models that mimic real construction vehicles—a piston-like action makes them move! Includes full-sized templates and assembly drawings for 8 display models.
ISBN: 1-56523-152-x, 144 pages, soft cover, $15.95

How-To Book of Birdhouses and Feeders
By Paul Meisel
This book features 30 Birdhouse and Feeder projects using common woodworking shop tools. Also includes information about attracting birds to your backyard.
ISBN: 1-56523-237-2, 208 pages, soft cover, $19.95

Birdhouse Builders Manual
By Charles Grodski, Roger Schroeder
Fill your backyard with practical and attractive birdhouses. Includes four start-to-finish projects, measured drawings, basic layout and wood information, and more than 50 finished examples.
ISBN: 1-56523-100-7, 108 pages, soft cover, $19.95

CHECK WITH YOUR LOCAL BOOK OR WOODWORKING STORE
Or call 800-457-9112 • Visit www.FoxChapelPublishing.com